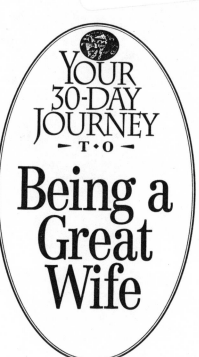

YOUR
30-DAY
JOURNEY
– T · O –

Being a
Great
Wife

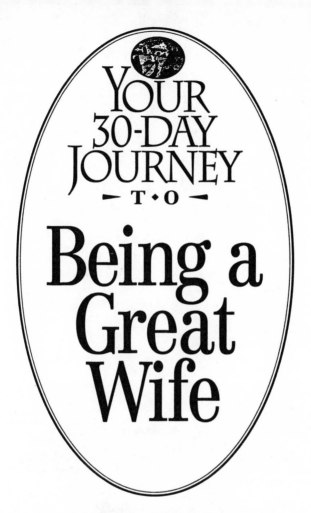

YOUR 30-DAY JOURNEY — T·O —

Being a Great Wife

PATRICK AND
CONNIE LAWRENCE

THOMAS NELSON PUBLISHERS
Nashville

Published in Nashville, Tennessee, by Oliver-Nelson Books, a division of Thomas Nelson, Inc., Publishers, and distributed in Canada by Lawson Falle, Ltd., Cambridge, Ontario.

The Bible version used in this publication is THE NEW KING JAMES VERSION. Copyright © 1979, 1980, 1982, Thomas Nelson, Inc., Publishers.

Printed in the United States of America.

ISBN 0-8407-9641-2

1 2 3 4 5 6 — 97 96 95 94 93 92

Contents

Introduction

Improving your marriage is an ongoing process that takes constant care. If you want to revitalize your marriage, the best place to start is within yourself. As you move through various stages of life, your marriage takes on new and changing qualities, requiring you to grow in becoming the best you can be in each season of life, in deepening your love for your husband, and in developing your skill at partnering with him. This book will guide you as you move toward being the best wife you can be at this moment.

If you choose to and are willing to take the necessary steps . . . you can be a great wife. This book will lead you as you explore what it means to be a great wife to your husband. You will find some markers to guide you as you make choices, effect immediate changes, and set long-range goals, which will lead you toward being the wife you want to be.

You might have started out in marriage with the secret hope you could change your husband into the man of your dreams. You might have thought, *There is enough here to work with, BUT . . . if only he were a little more considerate . . . if only he would stop drinking . . . if only he would talk more . . . if only he would pick up his socks . . . if only he would lose weight . . .* The list goes on and on. Perhaps without acknowledging it (even to yourself), you might have seen your job description as a wife prominently including the work of remodeling the man you married.

Since it's a BIG job to remodel another human being, you might not have taken time or emotional energy to focus on areas of your life that could use attention. You might have tried new and improved strategies to get him to change but over and over again faced frustration. When a woman focuses on trying to change a man, he may respond with distance or resistance, or he may try harder to change *her*. If you have tried to change your husband and are growing tired of the effort, this book represents a refreshing approach. You will now focus your energies of transformation where they will have a dramatic effect: in your life. You may not be able to change him into the man of your dreams, but you may wake up to ways of loving the real man you married that can make marriage to him even better than you dreamed possible.

You can't expect a total marital make-over in 30 days. However, if you will take the next 30 days to honestly consider what you can do in your life to make decisively positive changes, you will be amazed at the positive results. This book has no power to change you until you begin to participate. Your willingness to explore life, love your husband, and try some new ways (or refresh some old ways you've forgotten) will bring about the changes you're hoping for.

My sincere desire is that this book will become a memento of something wonderful you chose to do for yourself and your husband, a memento of experiences that helped you be a great wife in tangible ways. Years from now, when you find it tucked away behind a line of books or perhaps under a bed, may you smile with a sense of your own accomplishment.

P.S. If you are a husband about to buy this book for your wife, that's fine . . . as long as you also get the companion volume, *Your 30-Day Journey to Being a Great Husband!*

Making a Commitment to the Journey

Every journey involves a certain amount of work, the energy needed to get you from here to there. This journey is no different. To get where you want to be, you will need to expend your energies and abilities in the following ways: reading, rethinking your role and relationship, looking at yourself, changing your perspective, making new choices, adopting new attitudes, taking action, and reflecting on what you are learning and experiencing.

Each day's itinerary is set for you in general terms. You will make it apply to your particular situation. At every point along the way, you are free to choose your own level of involvement. You don't have to use all the information provided or do everything suggested. You may think of things not mentioned that would apply to your situation. You are free to add them to your itinerary. You move as much as *you* choose.

Completing the journey will take commitment on your part. Doing anything consistently for 30 days takes commitment, especially when you may be changing attitudes and habits. Each day's agenda will take at least thirty minutes, and you may find that you want to take more time than that, especially if you end up discussing the issues with someone. Beyond the time required, you will need to commit yourself to find courage to keep going when the personal evaluation and new ways of relating to your husband feel foreign or uncomfortable.

PERSONAL EVALUATION

Are you willing to make a 30-day commitment to your journey to being a great wife?

ACTION

My Personal Commitment

I, _____, am serious about my desire to be a great wife to my husband, *(his name here)* _____.

I am willing to invest at least thirty minutes a day, from each of the next 30 days, to focus on this journey. I will plan to take this time each *(circle one)* morning, lunchtime, afternoon, evening, or before bedtime.

I understand that to reach this goal, I must be willing to grow on a personal level, to exercise the courage to look at myself honestly, and to make choices to give of myself. I will do *my* best in all of these areas.

Since my goal is to be a great wife, not a perfect wife, in the next 30 days, I will not focus my attention on how far I fall short of being the ideal wife. I will focus my attention on *moving forward* from where I am today toward what I want to be.

I make this commitment to myself this _____ day of _____, 19_____.

_____
Signature

REFLECTION

This section encourages you to reflect on the day's journey, consider how you feel about it, and look for any insight that may help you proceed. You can choose to do this by talking it over with a friend, writing your personal reflections in a private journal, praying about it, or just taking a few minutes to quiet yourself enough to think about your reactions to each day's journey. Take a moment now to decide which of these means of reflection you prefer. You may want to choose a combination. There is no right or wrong way. What's important is that you do what works best to gain insight about your journey.

Take a few moments today to reflect on the commitment you have made and how you're feeling about beginning this journey.

ENCOURAGEMENT

Your willingness to commit yourself is the key element needed for you to be a great wife. Your choice to make this journey has already put your feet on the path of success.

FOOD FOR THOUGHT

One person with a commitment is worth one hundred who only have an interest.
—Mary Crowley

A Great Wife . . .
by Whose Definition?

Are you a great wife?

Are you sure?

Stop for a moment and consider these questions. You may find them difficult to answer because being a great wife is hard to define. Unless you have a clear definition of any goal, you will never be sure that you have reached it. You have the opportunity within the next 30 days to answer these questions with a resounding YES! You will do that by clarifying your definition of what it means for you to be a great wife, setting specific, measurable goals, and choosing to take action to reach those goals.

Let's look at the phrase "being a great wife" and see what it involves that makes it difficult to define.

Being

Your being and identity are at the heart of your estimation of yourself in this most intimate of roles. If you have a healthy self-image and have grown up learning to value yourself as a worthwhile person who has something to offer, you will find it easy to see yourself in positive terms whenever you consider various roles you play in life.

If you have a poor self-image and have trouble acknowledging that you are a person of infinite value and worth, you may find it difficult to say you are even adequate in fulfilling the role of being a wife. In this most intimate relationship your poor self-image may affect your relationship with your husband in numerous ways that leave you feeling like a failure as a wife and as a woman, even if your husband tells you otherwise. To be able to have confidence that you are a great wife, you need to take steps to build up a healthy self-image so that the person beneath the role is acceptable to you.

Great

This word is a subjective measure of quality. To be great, you must exceed what is merely mediocre. To know something is great, you must first clearly know what is adequate, expected, or acceptable. To have confidence that you are a great wife, you must first clarify your expectations of what is acceptable. The role of being a wife is quickly changing in our society. If you are looking to societal norms to give you a stable standard of measurement, you may find yourself on shaky ground. If you base your estimation on biblical or more traditional family guidelines, you will have a more stable standard of measurement, but you will still need to clarify your understanding of how to apply biblical principles to your life today.

The measure of greatness also depends on who you allow to participate in the judging. Different people will have varying standards. It is normal for you to want to please your husband, to talk to other women to gain understanding of how to love your husband and to get a sense of how well you are doing. You decide who is allowed to sit on your panel of judges. In most cases the two most important people to please are yourself and your husband.

However, some husbands will not acknowledge

women as great wives, even if they are, because of their own limited perspective. One man commented, "A great wife? There is no such thing! The two words don't belong together in the same sentence." He happens to be divorced. If your husband takes a cynical or a negative view, you simply don't let him have the final vote on how well you are doing. His lack of appreciation of how great you really are may be frustrating, but it need not stop you from being the best you can be in the relationship and having confidence. Who knows? Once you complete your journey, you just may change his mind.

Wife

What is a wife anyway? Looking up various words in the dictionary led me to words like *wedlock* and *matrimony*, which seem to have lost something in the translation to real life. The best definition of a wife I could piece together from dictionary definitions came down to these central elements: a *wife* is "a woman legally united to a man through an act of devotion of herself to the union."

The Bible gives God's perspective on what it means to be a wife, which goes beyond what *Webster's* has the authority to define. God says that when a woman becomes a wife, God Himself joins her together with her husband in a spiritual union. She is designed to be a helper suitable for her husband in a relationship meant to lead to the ultimate satisfaction of each partner. These general definitions will differ based on who you ask. Who you allow to define your role as a wife will determine what being a great wife means to you.

PERSONAL EVALUATION

- Do you see yourself as a person of value and worth?
- How does your self-image (positive or negative) affect your ability to see yourself as a great wife?
- Are you willing to take steps to improve your self-image in general terms to be able to be a great wife?
- What standard of measurement do you use as a basis for deciding where the line is drawn between being a good wife or being a great wife? God's? Your girlfriend's? Society's? Your mother's? Your husband's?
- Are you comfortable with the panel of judges you have allowed to influence how well you think you are doing in this area?

ACTION

Obtain a three-ring binder to use for keeping notes on your 30-day journey. On the first page, write out your own definition of what it means to be a great wife. You can talk to anyone you like and use any sources you like to help you come up with your definition. Later in the journey you will have some help in clarifying your definitions into specifics that will help you know when you have reached your goal of being a great wife.

Ask your husband to write out a definition of what he thinks it means to be a great wife and seal it in an envelope that he will hold until the end of your journey. At that time you can evaluate how well you have met your own goals and how you compare to your husband's definition of a great wife. You will be in a much more confident position at that point to be able to hear what he wants in a wife without being intimidated. At that point you can choose how to respond to his definition.

REFLECTION

Could you be a great wife, even if your husband never acknowledged it? If your definition of being a great wife completely depends on the approval of your husband, is it really a goal you can reach?

FOOD FOR THOUGHT

He who finds a wife finds a good thing,
And obtains favor from the LORD.
—Proverbs 18:22

Being a Great Wife ... The Choice Is All Yours

Being a great wife is a matter of choice, and the choice is all yours. No one else can make you a great wife, and no one else can keep you from being a great wife if that is what you decide to be. It is a matter of how you choose to employ your life and abilities. You can be a great wife regardless of whether your husband is a great husband or whether he will ever admit to what a great wife you are. His involvement can influence whether you have a great marriage, but you alone make the choices that determine whether you are a great wife.

The ingredients called for in being a great wife are quite common. You have the abilities it takes to be a great wife. You have the ability to know, help, love, encourage, build up, lend support, understand, touch, feel, express yourself, share your wisdom, affirm, appreciate, listen attentively, evoke trust, provide a safe haven, forgive, enjoy sexual intimacy, respect, admire, praise, honestly confront, persevere, show kindness, display affection, nurture, articulate what you need and want, and much more, depending on your individual gifts and talents. It is your choice as to whether you will devote your abilities to the purpose of being a great wife on a daily basis.

To devote or *dedicate* something means "to set it apart for a special purpose." When you choose to devote your life to a specific purpose, the act of devotion necessarily limits the focus of your life. Here is a common example of devotion. Let's say you want to devote a videotape for the purpose of recording your son's birthday parties as he grows up. From year to year you set this tape aside for this specific purpose. You add each annual celebration to create a special recording reflecting the living out of your initial purpose for which the tape was devoted. You choose not to use the tape for any purpose other than that for which it was set apart. If you did, the tape would lose something of its unique character and value in terms of being what it was chosen to be. Being a great wife is a matter of devotion.

Your life will be devoted to more than just being a wife to your husband. However, this act of devotion is the only one that dedicates the whole length of your life to another person. You will be dedicated to your children and friends, but the relationships are seasonal. There will come a time when children and friends move on in their own lives, and your purpose changes in relationship to them. If your marriage vows are fulfilled, you will be in union with your husband for the course of this natural life, and your purpose in relationship to him will not change. Therefore, your devotion to being a wife will take preeminence over other acts of devotion.

When you chose to dedicate yourself to being a wife, loving your husband and being his partner in life, you acted to define part of your chosen purpose for the course of your life. When you made that choice, you closed the door to other men, promising to keep yourself only unto him and forsaking all others until death. Your act of devotion also calls for closing the door to other uses of your life that would interfere with your devotion in marriage. That requires more than a one-time commitment. It is a commitment that needs to be guarded with every choice you make regarding where and how you apply your abilities, what your priorities are, what is the focus of your attention, and how you choose to spend your time and energy. Fulfilling your commitment of devotion to your husband makes you a good wife . . . but you can do even better.

You can be a great wife by fully embracing the commitment you have made and determining to give it your best every day. Being a great wife includes choosing to take a positive perspective toward your marriage, developing positive attitudes, and setting some goals that will take you beyond mediocrity to being the great wife you can be . . . if you so choose.

PERSONAL EVALUATION

- Are you blaming anyone but yourself if you do not see yourself as a great wife? Who?
- Are you willing to accept that you alone determine whether you are a great wife?
- To what have you devoted your life? (Include the roles you take seriously: wife, mother, friend, child of God, employee, employer, sister, business executive, and so on. Include any form of self-expression you are devoted to because it is an outlet for your unique talents: music, art, drama, athletics, writing, and so on.)
- Where do you experience conflict between any of the things to which you have devoted yourself and your primary devotion of yourself in marriage? (For example, is there a conflict between what it takes for you to be a great wife and to

fulfill your role at work or with your children? Are you devoted to other things that conflict with your devotion to your husband or cause you confusion when making decisions about the use of your time?)

- Are you willing to learn how to have a more positive perspective and attitude toward your marriage commitment?

ACTION

Title a page in your notebook "The Devotion of My Life." On this page, list items to which your life is devoted.

Next to each one, place a number noting the priority of importance it holds in your life. Dare to be honest. Don't put your role of being a wife first just because that is the focus of this book. In your own heart, at this very moment, which items mean the most to you? One way to judge relative importance is to see which ones win out over others when you have to decide how to spend your time, energy, and emotional reserves.

If you want to be a great wife, choose (as an act of your will) to make your devotion to your husband a top priority. If you don't know how to live out this devotion in specific terms, don't worry. Just continue on, choosing each day to honestly do your best in completing that day's journey.

REFLECTION

How does elevating your devotion to your husband to a top priority limit or change your involvement in each of the other items on your list?

ENCOURAGEMENT

By making the choice to devote yourself to being a great wife, you will say no to some good things, but you will say yes to the best in your marriage.

FOOD FOR THOUGHT

We must not, in trying to think about how we can make a big difference, ignore the small daily difference we can make which, over time, adds up to big differences we cannot see.

—Marian Wright Edelman

Setting Goals That Lead to Being a Great Wife

This 30-day journey is a positive part of a journey that never ends. You may already be a great wife. If you are, you will have a chance to gain confidence and polish up your virtues. This 30-day journey is a time for setting some specific short-term goals that will bring changes in your life-style; these goals then flow into the fulfillment of the ongoing goal of being a great wife. On Day 30, when you evaluate your progress and decide where you go from here, you will be in a better position to know what obstacles you face, what skills and knowledge you need to acquire, and what sources of help you need to reach the longer range goal of being a great wife for a lifetime.

Your first step to setting goals that lead to being a great wife requires that you clearly define your objective in measurable terms. Here is a general definition you can use to clarify your specific personal goals: *being a great wife involves your identity (being), your relationship (knowing and loving your husband), and your function (partnering with him in life).*

My idea of being a great wife, which includes identity, relationship, and function, is depicted in the three overlapping spheres of this diagram:

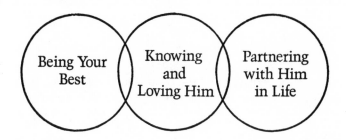

In the context of this journey you will be seeing yourself in these three primary areas: (1) becoming the best you can be, (2) strengthening your relationship with your husband by knowing and loving him, and (3) improving your partnering skills.

The body of this book focuses on specific ways you can grow in each of these areas. You will have the opportunity to make simple changes in each area that can make a great difference in your life and marriage. You can also use your knowledge of yourself and your husband to think of other things you can do that may not be included specifically in these categories but you tailor to the special needs in your marriage.

PERSONAL EVALUATION

- Of the three areas in the diagram, in which area would you say you have the most room for improvement?
- In which area do you feel the most confident?
- What are a few immediate short-term goals you can think of for each area?
- What are a few long-range goals (taking six months or more) you can think of for each area?

ACTION

Copy the diagram of the three areas that make up a great wife into your notebook. Rate yourself on a scale of one to ten for each sphere in terms of how well you believe you function in that category in general terms. (One is poor, five is adequate, and ten is excellent.)

Make three sections in your notebook: "Being My Best," "Knowing and Loving Him," and "Partnering in Life." On a sheet in each section, list three specific short-term goals you know would help you move toward being a great wife in that area. Also list three possible long-term goals that would help you in each area.

Take some action today to move toward doing one of the things you listed as a short-term goal in each area. For being your best, you might choose something as simple as taking a brisk walk. For knowing and loving your husband, you might write a love note. For partnering with him, you might ask him about a problem he is facing and offer to help in some way.

REFLECTION

How do you feel about evaluating yourself in terms of being a great wife?

There are real obstacles in life when we are dealing with human relationships. Consider what obstacles stand in your way as you move toward being a great wife. What keeps you from being your best? What keeps you from knowing your husband intimately? What keeps you from loving your husband whole-

heartedly? What keeps you from being a great partner in life?

ENCOURAGEMENT

If you continue to make daily choices to be your
best, devote yourself wholeheartedly to knowing and
loving your husband, and work toward the goal of being a great partner in life, you will be a great wife.

FOOD FOR THOUGHT

Take short steps. A lot of people fail because they try
to take too big a step too quickly.

—Zig Ziglar

The Benefits of Being a Great Wife

A story tells of a man who was given the opportunity to visit both heaven and hell. What he learned from this trip illustrates some of the benefits available from being a great wife.

When the man arrived in hell, he was quite surprised by what he saw. Instead of the expected fire and brimstone, he saw an enormous banquet table about five feet wide that extended as far as his eyes could see. There were people seated along each side. The banquet set before them was rich. The man was astonished to see an abundance of elegantly arranged fruits and vegetables. The aroma of fresh baked breads and pies wafted through the air, causing his mouth to water. Every imaginable type of meat, poultry, and fish, cooked to perfection, along with gravies and garnishes awaited the diners. At first the man was so overwhelmed by the banquet that he failed to notice the faces of the people seated at the table. Their faces were pitiful, hungry, scared, desperate.

When his attention turned to them, he was suddenly sobered by what he saw. Before each one was placed the foods the person most hungered for, but no one was eating. The great banquet was left untouched, although there was a great commotion around the table. A closer look revealed the reason for the commotion. The people were unable to bend their arms to serve themselves. Splints were attached to the inside of their arms so it was impossible to bend them at the elbows. Try as they would to lift the food they craved, they could never get it to their mouths. As the frustration mounted, people began to vent their anger at those near them. Fearing the others would take away the food they wanted, they began using their outstretched arms to batter one another. That was how they would spend eternity: always seeing before them what would feed their hunger but never being able to experience it; always fighting to make sure no one took away what they wanted but never getting what they desperately needed.

The man had seen enough. He asked to move on, eager to peer behind those pearly gates. Again he saw an enormous banquet table about five feet wide that extended as far as his eyes could see with people seated along each side. The banquet set before them was rich. It appeared to be identical to the lavish banquet table he had seen in hell. Before each one was placed what the person most hungered for. People were eating and enjoying themselves greatly.

What surprised the man was that here, too, people were unable to bend their arms to serve themselves. They, too, were limited with splints attached to the inside of their arms so they could not bend their elbows. The difference was that the people cared for one another. They asked those across from them what they wanted and needed from the banquet table. Each one chose to serve a partner. Each one took care to give the partner the particular foods desired, prepared in the way that suited the partner's tastes. There was no frustration as the people at the heavenly table listened to one another and acted to lovingly meet partners' needs. The food seemed to taste better to the one receiving it because it was served out of love.

The servers not only enjoyed what they were served but also enjoyed the part they played in making life heavenly for their partners. There was no fear of being deprived, no need for self-defense; the outstretched arms were not weapons. That was how they would spend eternity: always seeing what would feed their hunger before them, knowing that they could not nourish themselves as they needed to be nourished, but realizing others cared enough for them to get to know what they needed and reach out in love to bring it to them. They, too, knew the joy of being able to reach out to other persons in need and to give what the persons needed.

In this story and in marriage, the willingness to love, to listen, to recognize needs, and to extend yourself to meet those needs can make the difference between starvation and satisfaction, frustration and fulfillment, hell and heaven.

When you are a great wife, extending your life to understand and meet the needs of your husband, to serve him as a matter of choice and a demonstration of your love for him, you will benefit. There will be benefits in the atmosphere of your home, in the intimacy of your relationship with him, in the sense of self-respect you gain as you realize the level of fulfillment you can bring to another person's life by simple acts of love. There will also be benefits in terms of what you receive from him.

Being a great wife will no doubt be beneficial to your husband, but it cannot be something you do just for your husband. You need to have a clear vision of the benefits you will receive by being a great wife. In other words, what is in it for you? Envisioning the benefits you will receive by being a great wife gives you the internal motivation that will keep you moving, even if your husband is slow to notice the wonderful changes taking place within you. But be patient. In time his responses will come as he sees you genuinely devoting yourself to loving him.

PERSONAL EVALUATION

- Is the atmosphere in your marriage more like the banquet table in hell or the one in heaven? What parallels can you draw?
- Are you willing to extend yourself in ways that will meet your husband's needs?
- What are the needs within your life and marriage you are hungry for but unable to reach on your own? Do you think your willingness to reach out to meet your husband's needs may change the atmosphere so that your husband would be more inclined to reciprocate?
- What are the benefits you could imagine receiving when you are a great wife?

ACTION

In your notebook, list benefits you will gain from being a great wife. Some of them will take the form of the response you hope to get from your husband when he begins to appreciate the changes you make, and that is O.K. Be sure to list some benefits from being a great wife that do not depend on your husband's response, however. Some examples would be feeling more confidence, looking better, having improved self-image, enjoying better health, feeling less guilt, and so on.

REFLECTION

Some people say that what goes around comes around or that whatever you give out will always come back to you. The Bible says, "Give, and it will be given to you: good measure, pressed down, shaken together, and running over. . . . For with the same measure that you use, it will be measured back to you" (Luke 6:38). Consider how what you are receiving is related to what you have been giving out. Imagine what could happen when you change the measure you are giving out.

ENCOURAGEMENT

You will receive many benefits from being a great wife. As you focus your attention on loving your husband, you will find that your own life is enriched in the process.

FOOD FOR THOUGHT

What you get by reaching your goal is not nearly as important as what you become by reaching your goal.

—Zig Ziglar

Accept Responsibility for Your Life

All forms of positive change require accepting personal responsibility for your life. As long as you are abdicating responsibility for your wholeness, health, and/or happiness to your husband or anyone else, you will have great excuses but little power to create a better life.

When you accept responsibility for your life, you will see to it that your needs are being met from a variety of sources. When you are making choices and taking action to ensure you are nourished physically, mentally, emotionally, and spiritually, you will experience the kind of life that leaves you with something left over to share with others. Out of your sense of well-being and abundance, you will be able to give generously to your husband. When you responsibly care for yourself, you will not have to focus on trying to make others be what you need. Instead, you will be a refreshing well from which they can draw. You will feel like giving of yourself and be able to do so enthusiastically.

If you allow yourself to become depleted while waiting for someone else to meet your needs, you will end up at a deficit, always needy, grasping for whatever nourishment you are hungering for, growing in resentment toward whoever you believe owes you what you lack. When your life is not well cared for, you will have little to give and little energy or enthusiasm with which to give what you have. You will become a person who drains others of life and energy. When you are in this state of being, you can't be a great wife because your focus will always be on finding new ways to get someone to fill your deficit instead of giving of yourself the way a great wife must be able to do.

Everyone needs to beware the potential traps of irresponsibility, but that is especially true in marriage. When you join your life in the union of marriage, there is ample opportunity to shift the blame for your lack of fulfillment to your husband. Below are some common traps in belief and life-style that characterize failing to accept full responsibility for your life. Check to see if you may be stuck in any of them. If you are, get whatever help is necessary to break free.

Holding Faulty Beliefs

If you grew up believing in fairy tales, you might have accepted the myth that your husband was going to rescue you from the drudgery of life, transform you into a princess, and make you live happily ever after. If you sincerely believe that to be his responsibility, you may fail to accept responsibility for your life out of ignorance.

Playing the Victim

Lisa blames her lack of fulfillment on her husband, Ed. To hear her tell it, Ed just doesn't meet her needs. When they first got married, she expected him to make the loneliness disappear and give her a sense of personal fulfillment. At first Ed was really trying, but he never quite measured up. Lisa pointed out her needs, regularly noting where he failed to meet them. In reaction to the constant criticism, Ed withdrew. Lisa resorted to nagging, complaining, whining, berating, and begging. None of those tactics worked. Lisa is certain her problems and dissatisfaction in life are Ed's fault. She is so focused on seeing her husband as the source of her problems, she locks herself into a life of unfulfilled needs.

Acting Like a Dependent Child

Janice had always felt rather helpless. When Terry asked her to marry him, she could hardly believe her good fortune. Her mother was growing older, and Janice, at age twenty-eight, was wondering who was going to take care of her. Now she had Terry. When they were married, Janice transferred the responsibility for her life and happiness from her mother to her husband. Janice continued in the role of a dependent child. She looks up to Terry and down on herself. When he doesn't meet her needs in the way she expects, she becomes demanding, behaving like the irresponsible child she sees herself to be. If you have lived your life as a dependent child, you must begin the weaning process. Being a great wife requires that you behave as a mature adult.

Being Responsible for Everyone Else While Neglecting Yourself

From the time Amanda was small, growing up in a home where both parents were alcoholics, she found her identity in taking care of others. When she met Andrew, she saw how much he needed someone to take care of him. She knew he drank, but she felt sure that with her loving care, he could be induced to stay sober. After twelve years of marriage, Amanda is still taking care of him, trying to control his alcoholism, resenting that she spends her life giving endlessly without receiving the love she needs. She thinks of leaving but knows he couldn't live without her. Besides she feels at home in the relationship because he needs her so much. She looks down on her husband and elevates herself above him. Long ago she gave up living her own life. If you ask her what she wants and needs for herself, she probably won't know how to respond. She may avoid her own needs until she is utterly depleted. In time she may become bitter, angry, and resentful. If you relate to this situation, you need to release your husband to accept responsibility for his life and do the same for yourself. You may find helpful resources dealing with issues related to codependency.

If you want to be a great wife, accept responsibility for your life. That does not mean you become self-sufficient, pretending you don't need your husband. It means you become responsible to identify your needs and develop a network of friendships and support connecting you to people and resources that will nourish you. Your husband is certainly a key player in meeting your needs, but your life, wholeness, health, and happiness are your responsibility, not his.

When you accept your life and fulfillment as your responsibility, you can identify needs that you want your husband to meet for you. Once you have identified these needs, you can talk to your husband and let him know how important he is to your life in this particular way. You build him up and give him an opportunity to give to you as an act of love.

PERSONAL EVALUATION

- Who is responsible for your fulfillment, wholeness, health, and happiness in life?
- What do you blame your husband for in terms of your own lack of fulfillment?
- Do you see yourself falling into any of the irresponsibility traps? Which one(s)? What are you willing to do to get help in this area?
- Are you willing to accept the powerful role of taking personal responsibility for your life?

ACTION

This exercise will allow you to accept responsibility for each general area of your life. Title five sheets of paper in your notebook with these headings: "Physical Life," "Mental and Intellectual Life," "Spiritual Life," "Emotional Life," and "Financial Life." For each sheet, make columns across the top with these headings: "Needs"; "Me"; "My Husband"; "Other People"; "Other Resources."

List all of your needs you can think of in the "Needs" column. Place check marks in the appropriate column across the page, noting who you look to for meeting that need. If you depend only on your husband, you need to learn to consider other possible sources and what you could do to meet your own needs in that way.

REFLECTION

Consider how accepting responsibility for your life and personal fulfillment will change your attitude toward your husband in relationship to having your needs met. Consider what you might be afraid of when considering accepting full responsibility for your life.

ENCOURAGEMENT

Being personally responsible will free you and empower you to be a great wife. Even if you have never approached life this way before, try it for the remainder of this journey. It can beautifully revolutionize your life and relationships.

FOOD FOR THOUGHT

The finest thing a woman can offer a man is herself as an adult, someone who will hold him as well as be held.

—Sonya Friedman

Appreciate What You Have to Offer

Webster's Dictionary defines *appreciate* as "1, recognize the worth of; esteem duly. 2, be fully conscious of. 3, raise in value." Today you are going to
appreciate yourself and what you have to offer your
husband as a great wife.

To prepare a good resume, you reconsider all you
have to offer: background, knowledge, experience,
skills, understanding, attitude, special qualities, talents, personal attributes, character qualities, special
interests, and so on. You consider the requirements
and purpose of the job, along with everything you
know about the organization and the person making
the hiring decision. A good resume is a creative look
at yourself designed to convince the one doing the hiring that you are uniquely suited to the position you are
seeking to fill. For a resume to be effective, it should
be tailored to the needs of the sought-after position.

If you have ever had to update a resume to apply for
a new position or promotion, you might have had
this experience. You list all you have to offer, arrange
it attractively by highlighting the particular way
your qualities, abilities, and knowledge would fit the
bill. When you finish, you read it and marvel at how
much you have to offer. You become fully conscious
of aspects of your person and potential that might
have been taken for granted by yourself and others.
When you present your resume to the person consid-

ering you for the promotion, your value is raised in the person's eyes as well as in your own.

You are someone special with much to offer your husband in the position of wife. You have qualities, talents, special knowledge, skills, and attitudes that make you a prime candidate for being his lifelong helper, friend, lover, companion, motivator, confidante, and partner. You may be resting comfortably in your confidence that you are already hired for the position. Perhaps you are resting on your oars a bit. You may be bored with the assignment, and you continue your wifely routine without feeling inspired and creative in approaching all that being a wife can draw out of you. You probably fail to realize your tremendous value as a person and in terms of what you can do in the role of being a wife.

PERSONAL EVALUATION

Pretend your husband has amnesia and doesn't remember his wife. He has decided to accept resumes for the position followed by interviews for those he deems most suitable for his particular needs. You don't know who else is in the running, but you suppose there is competition and you are one of the applicants submitting a resume for the position. You are going to reconsider yourself and what your husband needs in a wife to create a convincing resume for the position. Here are some questions to consider in preparing the necessary information:

- What factors are of uppermost importance to him when considering his needs?
- What experience, background, knowledge, and education have prepared you for the position?

- What are your special talents and abilities?
- What skills have you developed that could be utilized in the position?
- What principles and beliefs have you built your life upon that give you strength to offer in the position?
- What personality traits and character qualities would enable you to be a positive member of his team?
- What positive difference can you make in his life if given the opportunity?
- What are your positive attitudes that would make you attractive as someone he would want to spend time with?
- What demonstrates that you are trustworthy?
- How can you relate each one of these aspects of what you have to offer to his unique needs, personality, and desires?

ACTION

Write a brief cover letter telling your husband why you want the position as his wife and asking for an interview.

Create a one-page resume with the following format, filling in a paragraph for each item listed. Rework each paragraph until you feel confident that you have presented the best you have to offer in the most convincing and attractive way possible.

Your Name

Objective: Being a great wife to _____

(your husband)

Education:
Experience:
Skills and Abilities:
Special Knowledge *(of him and the position)*:
Personal Attributes:
Attitude:
Character Qualities:
References:

REFLECTION

Think about what an interview for the position might be like, once your resume is chosen. Prepare yourself mentally to answer questions that are common in job interviews, such as What are your greatest strengths and weaknesses? What can you tell me about yourself? Why do you believe you could do this job well? How can I be sure you will stay in the position? (If your husband is agreeable to playing along with a positive attitude, set up an appointment for an interview and see where it leads.)

ENCOURAGEMENT

By thoughtfully playing along with this game, you will be able to see yourself in a fresh light. You will undoubtedly be surprised at how much you really do have to offer that you might have been taking for granted.

FOOD FOR THOUGHT

You are unique, and if that is not fulfilled, then something has been lost.

—Martha Graham

Take Care of Your Health and Appearance

When you take care of yourself physically, you are demonstrating love for yourself and your husband. Although you want him to love you for the person inside, the way you treat your body is a reflection of who you are inside and the level of respect you have for yourself.

There are many sensible reasons to take care of your health and appearance as they relate to being a great wife. Here are some of them:

- If you look better and feel better physically, you can't help feeling better about yourself. A good self-image will make you more comfortable in the marriage relationship.
- Good health will give you more energy to devote to the relationship and shared responsibilities.
- It is a tangible way to show your husband you care about things that are important to him.
- When you feel fit and attractive, sexual intimacy is more appealing and comfortable for you.

Here are some basic ways to take care of your health and appearance:

Exercise

For the sake of your sex life alone (not to mention your general health and well-being), there is plenty of motivational material to get you up and moving. A recent article in *Reader's Digest*, titled "Brighten Your Sex Life," noted that moderate exercise one hour a day, three times a week, can have a dramatic effect on a marriage. Several research studies cited in the article showed that people who exercised regularly experienced physiological changes that create a "sexual second wind," have more stamina, more easily ward off the blues by releasing endorphins (mood-elevating hormones) into the bloodstream, develop a better self-image, experience a significant jump in sexual confidence, feel more attractive, and have an increase in sexual desire and satisfaction after several months of exercising.

Sleep

Giving yourself the rest you need is a service to yourself and your husband. You must have enough sleep on a regular schedule if you are to function at peak performance. Lack of sleep can leave you irritable, fatigued, mentally impaired, and emotionally vulnerable.

Nutrition

If you are what you eat, eating a nutritious diet is an important part of being a great wife.

Preventive Health Care

Taking care of your health is a way of showing your love to those who love you. If you maintain a regular routine of preventive health care, you will be sick less often and may save your life. Since early detection is crucial to the survival rate in both cervical and breast cancer, your commitment to preventive health care may mean the difference between your husband's having you by his side to a rich old age or becoming a widower.

Physical Hygiene

Keeping your body, hair, teeth, skin, and nails clean and well-groomed affects the appearance and fragrance you bring to the world. Caring for yourself with good grooming habits makes you someone nice to be near.

Dressing Up and Making Up

Take care to dress attractively in neat, clean clothing. Choose clothes that are stylish, appropriate to the occasion, and in colors that best display your beauty. Use cosmetics in ways that make you feel more attractive and please your husband's sense of beauty.

PERSONAL EVALUATION

- Can you think of other reasons for taking care of your health and appearance?
- Do you get enough exercise and rest to be at your best each day?
- Is your diet nutritious and health preserving?
- What is your regular schedule of preventive health care?
- Do you practice good grooming habits on a daily basis? If you lack in this area, what part of your personal hygiene are you neglecting?
- Do you dress yourself in a way that brings out the beauty within you? Do you do the best you can with your resources? Do you dress up

for your husband as well as you dress up to present yourself to people you associate with outside your home?

ACTION

Rate yourself on a scale of one to ten for how well you take care of yourself in each of the following areas: exercise, sleep/rest, nutrition, preventive health care, physical hygiene, dressing up and making up. (One is poor; five is adequate; ten is excellent.)

Choose three specific things you are willing to change in your life-style to take better care of your health and appearance. You do not need to choose the three areas where you feel you need the most improvement; in fact, that may be self-defeating. Instead, make a commitment to achieve three small changes within your immediate reach. List these three items in the form of a commitment in your notebook. Tell someone who will be supportive of you and ask the person to hold you accountable to maintain these simple changes for the next twenty-one days.

If you have not had a physical checkup from a doctor in the past year, call today and make an appointment.

REFLECTION

The inability to care for yourself in these basic ways may indicate deeper issues that are affecting you and your marriage. Consider the ways you find it most difficult to take care of yourself, and ask yourself what is the real problem that creates the obstacle to your health and well-being. If you can't figure it out or resolve the problem, seek professional help from someone who can assist you in dealing with the deeper issues.

ENCOURAGEMENT

Your willingness to make positive changes in self-care will give you immediate results and make the rest of your journey more enjoyable. Do the best you can to be good to yourself.

FOOD FOR THOUGHT

A man falls in love through his eyes, a woman through her ears.

—Woodrow Wyatt

Set Boundaries of Self-Respect

A woman who respects her value as a human being first, a human being who has chosen to devote herself to being a wife, can be a great wife. She need not give up her personhood or any element of her dignity. It is a contradiction to try being a great wife while allowing yourself to be abused or treated as though you are not a respectable human being. How can you be a great wife if you allow the person within you to live a life of degradation?

In his book *Love Must Be Tough*, Dr. James Dobson focuses on the idea that self-respect is an essential factor in maintaining a healthy marriage. When you allow your boundaries of self-respect to be broken down through mistreatment, abuse, infidelity, or behavior that is degrading to your sense of human dignity, your marriage is weakened. When you learn to respect yourself and set up boundaries to limit what you will endure in relationship with your husband, you will become more attractive to him.

Here are some things you can do to establish and guard the boundaries of self-respect:

- Do take steps to recover from the experiences of life that have caused you to disrespect yourself. If you have suffered abuse, experience unhealthy shame, live with undue amounts of guilt, were raised to see yourself as worthless, or have endured severe losses and rejection, get the help you need to learn how to gain respect for yourself. You can find appropriate support groups, a professional counselor, spiritual guidance, or other resources to help you.

- Do treat yourself with respect by taking care of yourself, speaking well of yourself, and nurturing yourself.
- Do define for your children what behavior conveys respect and require them to display respect for you and your husband. Ask your husband to join with you in guarding the boundaries of respectful behavior within the family.
- Do set limits in your mind for where you draw the line in terms of unacceptable or degrading behavior.
- Do decide what you can do and where you can turn for help if you are ever faced with being treated abusively.

Certain behavior will destroy your self-respect and should be guarded against. Here are some guidelines for behavior you don't want to tolerate if you want to be a great wife:

- Don't accept physical abuse or threats of violence.
- Don't accept or tolerate known sexual infidelity.
- Don't accept dishonesty within the marriage relationship.
- Don't go along with behavior that is degrading to you or violates your conscience.
- Don't negate your true opinions, perceptions, feelings, needs, and concerns in an attempt to pretend to be the kind of person you think your husband wants you to be. He married you. Trust that there is much about you that he loves and

will respect if you dare to share your true self with him.

PERSONAL EVALUATION

- Do you respect yourself?
- How do you display self-respect in your everyday life?
- If you lack self-respect, what do you suspect as contributing factors to the way you feel about yourself?
- Are you willing to seek understanding and help so you can learn to practice self-respect?
- Do your children understand and practice respectful behavior in their family relationships?
- Are you currently enduring anything on the "don't list" in your marital relationship? Are you willing to seek help from someone who understands?

ACTION

Compile a list of the behavior and attitudes you consider generally outside the boundaries of respectful treatment. Think in terms of what no human being should have to endure from another, particularly within the marriage relationship. You are not necessarily describing conditions in your marriage.

List the things your husband does that display his respect for you.

List any areas where you feel violated or degraded by the behavior or attitudes of your children or husband. If you have never done so, discuss the matter with your husband, and let him know where you draw the line.

For each area of concern, plan something you can do to protect yourself from being violated in the future.

If you are in an abusive situation where it might be dangerous to discuss these issues openly, call someone today who can help you. Check with local churches, social services, women's organizations, or treatment centers.

REFLECTION

Self-respect begets respect from others. Degradation sets up a cycle of self-degradation. Consider how the cycle of self-respect or self-degradation is operating in your life. Are you moving toward greater self-respect? Are you blaming your husband for not giving you respect when you have not given yourself respect? What can you do to keep the cycle moving in a positive direction?

ENCOURAGEMENT

You can choose to make changes that will create greater self-respect and cause others to respect you more as well. When you dare to draw the line at the mark of self-respect, you will pave the way to being a great wife.

FOOD FOR THOUGHT

No one can make you feel inferior without your consent.

—Eleanor Roosevelt

Choose to Go Beyond
His Expectations

In every marriage, a husband and a wife will make certain demands of each other. When that happens, you can maintain your freedom of choice and a positive attitude by choosing to go beyond your husband's expectations.

Here's the example to follow. In Palestine, at the time of Christ, the nation of Israel was occupied by the Roman army. The law of Rome dictated that any Roman soldier could demand a Jew to carry his belongings as far as one mile. Most Jews rebelled against the symbol of subservience and would grudgingly go a mile with a soldier only upon demand and under threat of severe punishment. Jesus taught His followers to go beyond expectations. He suggested the revolutionary idea that they go a second mile, of their own free will, when the soldier's demands were met. This determination to display love by going the second mile changed their attitude. The second-mile intention in the heart turned the first-mile attitude from a grumble to a grin. The first mile, they fulfilled obligation; the second mile, they displayed love. The first mile, the soldier was in control; the second mile, Jesus' followers were.

You can apply this same powerful principle to your marriage by choosing to go beyond your husband's expectations. You can choose to display second-mile love to your husband.

PERSONAL EVALUATION

- What expectations did your husband bring into marriage about what you are supposed to do for him?
- Which of these expectations do you fulfill to keep the peace but do so grudgingly?
- Are you willing to make the choice to go beyond his expectations?

ACTION

Divide a sheet of paper into two columns. Write "First Mile" over the left column and "Second Mile" over the right column. List ten items in the "First Mile" column that your husband expects of you and gets upset if you do not comply with. In the "Second Mile" column, think of a creative way you can fulfill his expectations and dramatically exceed them in a way he would be sure to notice.

Pick three of these items and commit yourself to going beyond his expectations with a positive and loving attitude. Don't announce your intentions; just do it and note his response. Also notice how your feelings change as you practice going the second mile.

REFLECTION

Imagine yourself doing each of the ten items on your "Second Mile" list. Imagine the possible change in your attitude and the atmosphere of your home.

ENCOURAGEMENT

Practicing second-mile love can make your life and marriage much more enjoyable. Try this way of life awhile and see for yourself the positive difference it can make.

FOOD FOR THOUGHT

Grumbling is the death of love.
—Marlene Dietrich

Renew Your
Wholehearted Commitment

Most couples enter into marriage with a whole-hearted commitment. Even though statistics predict that 50 percent of marriages won't stand the test of time, you were probably confident that the two of you were going to make it. You said "till death do us part" and meant it, excitedly anticipating the life you would share. You committed yourself wholeheart-edly to loving, honoring, and cherishing, keeping yourself only unto him and forsaking all others, for better or for worse, in sickness and in health, for richer or for poorer.

With the future together bursting with possibili-ties, your hopes were high. As time passes you may find that life together is not what you expected. You may discover painful secrets you had not figured on when making your marriage commitment. You may suffer the death of shared dreams, have your trust in him severely shaken, experience loneliness or a lack of fulfillment in the relationship. You may have to grapple with the painful aftermath of infidelity. You may have to cope with the worse instead of the bet-ter, the sickness instead of the health, and being poorer rather than richer. In all of these cases and many others, you may develop reservations and es-cape hatches that translate into having something less than a wholehearted commitment to the union you promised to nurture for the rest of your life.

Being unwilling to divorce does not mean that you are wholeheartedly maintaining the commitment you made on your wedding day. You might have determined that no matter what, you were never going to divorce. Studies show that making a lifetime commitment is a primary determining factor in the success of any marriage, and you are determined to be successful. So, no matter what happens, you are in the relationship for life. But is your heart fully in the relationship, or have you withdrawn your whole heart out of a need for self-protection or a desire for revenge?

The wedges between you may be valid attempts at healthy self-preservation. The way to maintain a wholehearted commitment to your husband is not to ignore betrayals and disappointments or pretend things are other than they are. The wedges between you need to be addressed individually and dissolved through concerted efforts from both partners.

Whatever your marital experience, if you want to be a great wife, you need to choose your husband again today and each day of your life. A wholehearted commitment sometimes takes courage, especially if there has been deceit or infidelity. You can weigh your choices, and if you are going to stay in the marriage, choose to love him with a whole heart.

PERSONAL EVALUATION

- What has happened in your marriage that has caused you to hold back from wholehearted involvement? What hurts still need healing? What losses still need grieving? What betrayals still remain unforgiven? What areas of trust need to be rebuilt? What fears need to be faced and overcome?

- Do you have escape hatches prepared in case your marriage doesn't work out? How does the maintenance of these escape hatches affect your wholehearted commitment of yourself to your marriage today?
- Are you in your marriage today because you don't want to go through a divorce or because you have a wholehearted commitment to the relationship?

ACTION

List your reservations, what you hold back of yourself from the relationship. (They could be sexual vulnerability, finances, kindness, information you keep from him, and so on.)

List the issues that have become wedges between you and your husband. After each one, answer yes or no to whether the two of you can dissolve it on your own. If you have been trying without success, answer no. Although you want to dissolve the wedge, you may need outside help to accomplish that.

Choose your husband again today. Recommit yourself to him as an act of your will, to give your marriage all you have to offer. Choose to deal with whatever is causing you to withhold yourself from your husband. Choose to get help dissolving the wedges that have developed between you and your husband. If your husband is unwilling to seek help, choose to seek help on your own so that for your part the commitment can be wholehearted.

Reaffirm your love and commitment to your husband with words. Either tell him or write him a note. Don't focus on your areas of reservation if there are any. Just tell him that you love him, are committed to him for life, and are choosing today to reaffirm your commitment of love for a lifetime.

REFLECTION

Take some time to look at your wedding photographs and recall the quality of your commitment at that time. Think of the ways your commitment was lived out during your first year of marriage. Think of ways you can rekindle the spirit of love your commitment took when the relationship was young. Consider how enduring the difficulties of life together has made your mature commitment an even greater declaration of love.

ENCOURAGEMENT

By choosing him again today you will breathe fresh life and energy into your marriage.

FOOD FOR THOUGHT

A successful marriage is an edifice that must be rebuilt every day.

—André Maurois

Dump the Man of Your Dreams

While going through premarital counseling, one couple discovered the bride-to-be didn't have a clue to the identity of the real man she was about to marry. As a part of the counseling process, Anita and Donald took the Taylor-Johnson Temperament Analysis Inventory. This inventory asks questions about how you would act and feel in various situations. You answer each question twice—once for how you would act, and once for how you anticipate your partner would act. The results are plotted on a graph describing various temperament qualities on a continuum between opposite poles (like introverted and extroverted). When the results are presented, the counselor superimposes the results of what you think your partner is like with what the test reveals he is really like in terms of how he says he would act in real-life situations.

Anita was shocked to see that although Donald had predicted her responses to life with amazing accuracy, her view of what Donald was like bore no noticeable resemblance to the real man. The counselor spent some time helping Anita see that if her marriage were going to work, she would need to dump the man of her dreams, learning to know and accept the man she was about to marry.

Your image of your husband will need to be altered if you have superimposed a transparency of all your childhood dreams of what you hoped for in a husband over the real man. When you have an image of an ideal husband firmly envisioned in your mind, it's easy to see the real man in the image as you would like him to be. During courtship, your desire to get to know the real man might have been further hindered because your intended was probably on his best behavior, trying to please you and be the kind of man you desired.

When you discover the difference between the man of your dreams and the real man you married, you have to make a choice. You can continue to measure him against your ideal, comparing him to what you had always hoped for in a husband and trying to transform your frog into a prince by sheer willpower and determination. Or you can dump the man of your dreams, enjoy the adventure of getting to know and love the real man you married, learn to accept and appreciate the unique human being God created him to be.

If you insist on measuring him against your fantasy man, you will depreciate his unique personality and special qualities. You'll see what he is not and miss all that he is. That is a tremendous loss.

PERSONAL EVALUATION

- Do you find yourself noticing what disappoints you about your husband more than what you appreciate about him?
- Do you like your husband for who he is?
- Do you find that you are often surprised by his choices and actions?
- Do you have a hidden agenda of how you want to mold your husband into the man of your dreams? When you try to change him in these ways, what response do you get from him?

ACTION

Make a list of all the ways you would like to change your husband if it was in your power to do so. Put a check next to the items you actively try to change in him.

Look at each item on your list, and decide if you are willing to release the responsibility for change in that area back to your husband. If you are willing, cross that item off your list. For the items remaining on your list, ask yourself why you refuse to accept your husband as he is in this way. What does it threaten in you? Consider discussing these issues with a marriage counselor if they are recurrent areas of contention within your marriage.

Choose to dump the man of your dreams. Give up your crusade to change your husband into your version of Prince Charming. Instead, focus your attention on getting to know and like him for who he is.

Play this game to discover how well you know the real man you are committed to loving. Write the answer to each of the following questions with regard to your husband. After you have finished, ask him to answer the questions verbally, and see how well you know the real man you married.

- What are his favorite food, color, musical artist, TV show, movie star, political figure, and clothing outfit?
- What are three actions that speak love to him?
- What quirks do you have that bug him?
- What was the happiest day of his life? The saddest day?
- What are his height, weight, and eye color?

- Where are there scars on his body, and how did they get there?
- If he could, what would he change about his appearance, his past, his job, his marriage, his home?
- On a scale of one to ten, how would he rate the level of hope he feels for his future fulfillment of his dreams? (One is none; ten is a tremendous amount of hope.)
- What three concerns or worries are uppermost in his mind at the moment?
- What is his primary project at work currently?
- What are three things he most fears?
- Who are three of his heroes or people he admires?
- What was his favorite subject in high school and why?
- What does he consider his greatest personal strength? His greatest personal weakness?
- What are his talents that are not currently being used as much as he would like?
- What was his most embarrassing moment?
- Who does he see himself competing with at this stage of life? What is he competing for? How does he feel he measures up to the competition?
- What does he feel most guilty about?
- What are three of his favorite interests and/or hobbies?
- What special recognition has he received or award has he won? What does he believe deserves recognition that he has not been recognized for?
- What was his proudest moment?
- What are his religious beliefs about heaven and hell, the character of God, how God sees him,

and sin and forgiveness? What does he wish he could be sure of about God that he doesn't yet understand?

• What are the five major losses he has experienced in his life? Has he ever gotten over them or grieved them fully? Why or why not?

• What would he want written on his tombstone?

REFLECTION

Saying to your husband, "I like you," is very different from saying, "I love you," but every bit as important. How do you let him know you like him as well as love him?

If you have depreciated the real man you married by negatively comparing him to some ideal, consider whether an apology is in order.

FOOD FOR THOUGHT

This is one of the miracles of love: It gives . . . a power of seeing through its own enchantments and yet not being disenchanted.

—C. S. Lewis

Create a Sensational Atmosphere

Marriage involves all of your senses. In fact, it is through your senses that you communicate with each other. Although marriage is a spiritual union as well as a physical one, even the most profound spiritual aspects of life must be communicated through the senses: hearing, sight, smell, taste, and touch. The way you use your eyes, ears, nose, mouth, hands, and body can make a tremendous impact on your marriage. The things you do to please your husband's senses will create a sensational atmosphere for sharing love within your marriage.

One other component is essential to creating a sensational atmosphere for your marriage. It does not relate directly to any one of your physical senses. It has more to do with your mind and your will. It touches your husband to the depths of his heart. It is the choice to create an atmosphere of absolute trust and safety within your relationship. The Bible says,

Who can find a virtuous wife?
For her worth is far above rubies.
The heart of her husband safely trusts her;
So he will have no lack of gain (Prov. 31:10–11).

Start thinking of all the ways you can use your body and senses to love your husband. Here are some ideas:

Eyes

Look into his eyes whenever he is speaking to you; flirt with your eyes; listen with your eyes; see the good things he does. Apply cosmetics in a way he finds attractive.

Ears

Listen attentively; notice the inflection used when he is speaking; listen for the feelings beneath the words. Wear pretty earrings he enjoys seeing in colors that brighten your countenance.

Nose

Notice and appreciate the smell of him, his body, his cologne, the food he cooks or gives to you. Be aware of odors and fragrances in your environment.

Mouth

Smile. Speak words of kindness, encouragement, understanding. Keep it shut when he is talking, when tempted to divulge a confidence or tear him down. Kiss him passionately or tenderly. Wear an attractive shade of lipstick.

Head

Think before you speak or act. Nod while listening to him. Face him when he is speaking to you. Take care of your face and hair so you present your best appearance.

Hands

Make things he enjoys. Give him a pat on the back. Hold hands with him. Rub his back. Touch him sexually in ways most pleasing to him. Help lift the burdens and clean up the messes you face together in life. Extend your hands to his friends. Massage his tired feet. Wave to him. Groom your hands and nails so they are beautiful and pleasing to touch.

Arms

Welcome him home. Hold him. Bring him things he needs. Let him go when necessary.

Legs and Feet

Walk with him. Go places together. Go places for him. Stand together. Keep your legs and feet well-groomed and well-exercised.

Start thinking of all the ways you can create an atmosphere that is pleasing and stimulating to his senses. Here are some ideas:

- Create wonderful fragrances: potpourri, perfume, bath powder, baked bread, fresh ground coffee, fresh flowers, roast turkey. Guard against odors with cleanliness, and care for what you allow into your shared environment.
- Create visual beauty. Dress attractively; use colors and cosmetics to brighten your appearance. Decorate your home and surroundings in ways pleasing to the eye. Use your artistic talents (draw, paint, redecorate, update your wardrobe). Guard against clutter, disorder, and darkness.
- Create great feelings. Draw him a hot bath on a cold night. Surround him with soft blankets. Give him a rubdown with a velvet glove. Run your fingers through his hair.
- Fill the air with sounds he loves to hear: music and soothing sounds of ocean waves or waterfalls. Let him hear your laughter and the laugh-

ter of your children. Enjoy moments of silence. Say, "Well done."

- Let him taste the good things in life. Share some chocolate. Make his favorite meal. Give him an ice cold glass of lemonade on the hottest day of summer. Try new taste treats together.

Start thinking of ways you can create an atmosphere of trust and safety in the relationship. Here are some ideas:

- Never speak evil of him to your children or relatives.
- When he tells you something private, keep it to yourself.
- Never purposely deceive him.
- When he shares his struggles, listen attentively, ask questions to give you greater understanding, and be supportive. Don't tell him he is handling it all wrong.

PERSONAL EVALUATION

- What do you already do to create a sensational atmosphere in your marriage?
- What parts of your being could be better used to show love to your husband?
- Does your husband have good reason to say his heart can safely trust in you?

ACTION

List three things you are willing to do to use your body and senses to show love for your husband. Do one of them today.

List three things you are willing to do to create an atmosphere that is pleasing and stimulating to his senses. Do one of these things today.

If you have done things in the past to cause him not to be able to safely trust in you, list them and decide if you are willing to change your ways.

Write a statement of commitment listing the promises you will make to your husband so that his heart can safely trust in you.

Plan a special time to discuss this issue with your husband and share your new commitment with him.

REFLECTION

How can creating a sensational atmosphere for your husband enrich your life at the same time?

ENCOURAGEMENT

Take a fresh look at the quality of your life. By choosing to involve all of your senses in your endeavor to love your husband, the quality of your life will greatly improve.

FOOD FOR THOUGHT

No one can bestow a bouquet of flowers in the name of love without enjoying the beauty and fragrance.

Display Respect for Him and His Work

If you want to be a great wife, you must see to it that you respect your husband. You may love him with all your heart, but if love is not accompanied with respect, it may become a burden and an embarrassment to him. I think of the play *Funny Girl*. Fanny Brice, an unattractive girl from humble beginnings, finds fame and fortune performing with comedic flair in the Ziegfield Follies. She falls in love and marries Nicky Arnstein, a handsome, flamboyant gambler and successful businessman. As his financial empire begins to crumble while hers soars, she attempts to show her love for him by arranging a business deal designed to make him look good. When he discovers that his latest business venture is a pretense, he is outraged and terribly humiliated. He sees her act of love as a display of disrespect for him as a man and for his ability to succeed at work. This one issue spells disaster for their marriage, which ends in divorce.

Your husband needs your respect as well as your love. To respect him, you regard him highly, esteem him, and notice specific qualities that are praiseworthy. There is a fundamental difference between love and respect. Love says a lot about the person giving it. You can bestow love on anyone, regardless of worthiness, without necessarily approving of the person in any way. Respect implies more about the one receiving it than the one giving it. Respect is directly related to specific qualities in the recipient that you find remarkable.

Showing respect for your husband's work is also important. A man's work is much more than a means of gaining an income. It is an expression of his identity, a means of carving out his place in the scheme of things. It is his scorecard to help him decide whether he is making it in life, an expression of his love for his family, a display of his abilities and education, a means of finding a sense of belonging in the world, an attempt to gain a sense of significance, an opportunity for accomplishment. A man's work is his way of trying to reach the good life or a path to fulfilling his dreams.

Men tend to judge one another and themselves on the basis of occupation. A man's identity is intricately interwoven with what he does for a living. When men meet one another for the first time, they usually ask, "And what do you do?" That is their way of identifying status, gaining a handle on the other's identity, and judging the potential for relationship.

Women sometimes forget that a man sees his worth in light of his occupation. You may protest, "But my husband is much more than what he does!" True, he is more than what he does, but what he does—and the respect he receives for what he does— weighs heavily when measuring his self-worth. If you show disrespect for his work, which is for him a tangible measure of his value, he is not likely to share the rest of his being with you for fear of rejection.

If you have a view of life that places your husband or his work at the bottom of some social hierarchy, you need to change your perspective. There is good in every man, even if some things about him are not respectable. Look to find what is good and applaud it. Every job that is done to the best of one's ability is worthy of respect. Look to see the effort and attitude with which your husband does his job, and respect them. Here are some ways you can display respect for your husband and his work:

- Speak well of him, noting specific behavior, qualities, skills, and abilities you admire.
- Compliment him to others. Tell others what you are proud of in his life and work.
- Don't sit idly by and allow others to criticize him in your presence. Instead, come to his defense, sighting positive things about him. If you hear your children speaking disrespectfully of him, let them know that is not acceptable.
- Don't belittle his attempts at success just because they don't always succeed. Instead, praise his effort and the strengths and talents he used in the pursuit of success.
- Express interest in the projects he is working on. Ask him what it takes for him to successfully complete a project.
- When he has work duties that occasionally interfere with your plans or take him away from home, respect the pressure he is under to perform at work. If he must do something to fulfill his work-related duties, refrain from badgering him. Try to appreciate that it can be difficult to balance home and work, and that the work he does is partially for your benefit.
- Comment on your appreciation of the benefits

his work provides for your family. For example, when a child is sick and you have to use the medical benefits from his work, mention how secure you feel because your family is protected in that way.

PERSONAL EVALUATION

- Do you respect your husband? How do you show your respect?
- Do you respect the work he does and what he brings to his work? How do you show your respect?

ACTION

List ten things you respect in your husband as a person. These would be character qualities.

List ten things you respect in terms of good choices your husband has made in life.

List ten things related to the work your husband does that you respect.

List ten things you can do to show respect for your husband and his work.

Drawing from these lists, write your husband a letter expressing your respect for him. Give him the letter.

REFLECTION

How do you think your display of respect for your husband or your lack of respect affects your husband's self-image? His willingness to open up to you? His willingness to take risks?

ENCOURAGEMENT

Showing respect is a choice rather than a feeling. Your choice to respect your husband will have far-reaching positive effects on every other aspect of your life together.

FOOD FOR THOUGHT

Nevertheless let each one of you in particular so love his own wife as himself, and let the wife see that she respects her husband.

—The Apostle Paul

Appreciate Him

Rayna had a funny feeling something was wrong. There was no logical reason to worry, and yet something was gnawing at her. It was two days before Christmas, and in the midst of holiday happiness she felt terribly uneasy. She told herself Larry was probably late getting home because he had stopped to do some last-minute shopping . . . that's all it was. She smiled to herself at how he always tried to surprise her with a special Christmas gift but always waited until the last minute and then dashed madly about on Christmas Eve to find the perfect gift. Maybe this year he had decided to do his mad Christmas dash for her gift a day earlier. That thought consoled her for another forty minutes. When she couldn't shake off the uneasiness, she called his office.

"Hello, is Larry still there?" The voice at the other end was halting, "Well . . . um . . . there's been an accident . . . I mean a problem . . ." She heard nothing else for that one endless moment. She knew it. Hadn't she sensed that something was wrong? "Is he dead?" she heard herself blurt out the awful question. "No. He's O.K. I mean he's shaken but not hurt. He was robbed at gunpoint."

Apparently, Larry had been approached in the parking lot by a man who demanded his wallet. When he told the man that he wasn't carrying any money, the man lifted the gun to his temple. Larry said, "Look," turning his pockets out to reveal that they were empty. "All I have is my watch and my wedding ring." In the instant that meant life or death for Larry, the gunman decided to take the watch and ring and leave Larry with his life.

Christmas that year was lived in a different light. Each moment for the next few days and weeks, Rayna could not help thinking how life would be different if Larry was not alive to share it. She began to appreciate everything about him and the life they shared. Things she had grown to take for granted became noteworthy. She wasn't focusing on what he *didn't* do that she thought he should. She wasn't depreciating him as compared to other men. In remembrance of how fragile life can be, she developed a fond sense of appreciation for her husband.

In her book *What Every Woman Ought to Know About Love and Marriage*, Dr. Joyce Brothers suggests a game for women who are bored and dissatisfied with their husbands. She calls it the Widow Game. She explains,

> You pretend that your husband is dead. As of this minute you are a widow. And you are going to be a widow for a week. . . .
>
> When you wake up tomorrow morning, pretend that he is not lying there beside you. You have no one to talk to. You drink your coffee alone. In the course of the day, you are to do all the things you usually depend on him to do. . . .
>
> Don't cheat by telling yourself that if he were not in your life, there would be someone else, someone more stimulating, more attractive, someone sexier.

"Once the week is over," she concluded, "let yourself rejoice that you are not a widow, that he is still there beside you sharing your life. Be grateful for all those things you don't have to do by yourself. And show your gratitude. You will see him through rosier spectacles."

PERSONAL EVALUATION

- Have you fallen into the rut of taking your husband and the role he plays in your life for granted?
- Would you say that you fully appreciate your husband and let him know it?
- If asked, which do you think your husband would say you do more: appreciate him or depreciate him?

ACTION

Play the Widow Game as described by Dr. Brothers. At the end of the week, make a list of everything you appreciate about your husband.

REFLECTION

How do you think learning to appreciate him will give you a more positive attitude about your life?

ENCOURAGEMENT

Appreciating the man you married will allow you to enjoy your life more fully and will give him a boost at the same time. Choose to appreciate your husband.

FOOD FOR THOUGHT

Our expectancies not only affect how we see reality, but also affect reality itself.

—Edward E. Jones

Water the Seeds of Greatness Within Him

Every man has the seeds of greatness within him. A great wife takes note of where the seeds of greatness are buried in the life of her husband and waters them until they grow to be apparent to everyone and begin bearing fruit.

Just as seeds are buried under mounds of dirt, the seeds of good character qualities in a man may be buried under mounds of a different kind of dirt. The seeds of honesty may be buried under feelings of inadequacy and the fear of being rejected as he truly is. The seeds of kindness may be buried under his perceived need for rough walls of defensiveness. The willingness to work hard and the ability to achieve may be just beneath the surface of past failures and discouragement. Loyalty may have been trampled in the dirt of betrayal, hidden beneath a mistrust of others. Intelligence may be under the rock of a belief, drilled into him as a child, that he is witless.

You can water the seeds of greatness within him in several ways.

- Assume that he has great potential and good character qualities that can be developed.
- Look to discover what may be burying the seeds of greatness in his life. Which of his beliefs hold him down? What hurts has he experienced that cause him to doubt himself or others? Where has he tried and failed in the past? What conclusions

is he drawing about himself on the basis of the dirt he has experienced in life?

- Notice good qualities in seed form. If he tells you the truth when it would have been easier to evade the truth or misrepresent it, let him know that you appreciate his honesty. If he tries at something, even though he may not get the results he hoped for, praise the strength of his effort and what he did right. Point to his intelligence in action. Mention his smart choices, and comment on his wise perceptions.

- Water his seeds of greatness with words of encouragement. Tell him that he can grow and change for the better in ways he wants to grow. Tell him that you believe in him and his ability to learn new ways of life. Tell him that you know he has what it takes, his talents are worth developing, his love will be received and reciprocated, his hard work will pay off in time, his failures and disappointments are cobblestones on the path to ultimate success.

Although personal growth will be the outcome of watering the seeds of greatness within him, be careful not to use this tactic as a means to manipulate him into changing in the ways you want him to change. Be careful to honestly note what you see within him as a unique individual rather than make things up along the lines of what you would like in your ideal husband.

PERSONAL EVALUATION

- Do you assume your husband has seeds of greatness within him?

- Do you water those seeds with words of encouragement or plow them under with words of criticism?
- What is some of the dirt of life you suspect may be burying the seeds of greatness within your husband?

ACTION

Title a sheet of paper "Seeds of Greatness Within My Husband." On the left side, list positive qualities, talents, abilities, and potential you see in your husband. Across the page, on the right side, cite one example of how you have seen this in seed form within his life. Keep going until you have at least ten items on the page. If you can find more, keep writing for up to thirty minutes.

Look for opportunities when you can take note of, comment on, and encourage these seeds of greatness within him. As the opportunities naturally arise, water the seeds of greatness you have listed by mentioning what you notice to your husband and telling him what you think is so great about him.

REFLECTION

Think about a time when your belief in your husband and your encouragement of him gave him the courage to grow. Consider how your attitude about him can either nourish positive growth or stamp it out.

ENCOURAGEMENT

It is wonderful to realize that you play a major role in bringing out the best within your husband. Don't let a critical attitude keep you from seeing him grow into the man he was meant to be.

FOOD FOR THOUGHT

Marriage is a partnership in which each inspires the other, and brings fruition to both.
> —Millicent Carey McIntosh

Practice Good Communication Skills

"I know you believe you understand what you think I said, but I'm not sure you realize that what you heard is not what I meant." This comment from an anonymous source exemplifies how complicated simple communication can become, even when you are doing your best to understand. All good communication takes practice and skill. In developing good communication between husband and wife, another element comes into play, making the process even more of a challenge. This added element is the need to understand the frame of reference from which your spouse interprets what you are saying.

In the number one national best-seller *You Just Don't Understand: Women and Men in Conversation*, Deborah Tannen, Ph.D., says, "Talk between women and men is cross-cultural communication." She explains that because men and women engage the world in different ways, they also use words differently. Neglecting to take the differing communication styles into account may leave both of you hurt and bewildered, even though each of you did your best to communicate clearly and understand what the other was trying to say.

Dr. Tannen notes that many men engage the world as an individual in a hierarchical social order in which he was either one-up or one-down. In this

world, conversations are negotiations in which people try to achieve and maintain the upper hand if
they can, and protect themselves from others' attempts to put them down and push them around.
Life, then, is a contest, a struggle to preserve inde-
pendence and avoid failure.

In commenting on the way many women communicate, she writes that women engage the world

as an individual in a network of connections. In this
world, conversations are negotiations for closeness
in which people try to seek and give confirmation
and support, and to reach consensus. They try to
protect themselves from others' attempts to push
them away. Life, then, is a community, a struggle to
preserve intimacy and avoid isolation. Though there
are hierarchies in this world too, they are hierarchies more of friendship than of power and accomplishment.

A common example of the frustration that arises
from not understanding these differing perspectives
may occur when you try to share your feelings about
a problem with your husband. You are looking for intimacy, closeness, and support. You want to know he
is with you, to hear his confirmation that your troubled feelings are valid. From his perspective, where
life is a contest, your problem may be seen as a challenge to be conquered. You share feelings in hopes of
greater closeness. He responds with a solution to fix
the problem and win the contest. Once he has of-
fered the solution, he expects the discussion to be
over. The problem is solved, end of conversation . . .
right? Wrong! You didn't want him to solve it. You

wanted him to share it. When you continue the conversation, he may be offended that you rejected his solution. By his way of thinking, your ongoing talk of how you are feeling about the problem comes across as a put-down, demonstrating that he failed in his attempt to fix things. By your way of thinking, his simple dismissal of your feelings (just because there is a solution) disconnects you from him. Sharing a problem you felt so deeply about was an opportunity for intimacy. You may interpret his dismissal of the problem to mean that you and your feelings have been dismissed, also.

A great wife will learn to be a good cross-cultural communicator. You can do that by educating yourself on issues related to male-female communication and practicing skills basic to all good communication. Some of these skills are outlined below along with a few tips on things you can practice.

1. Sending a Clear Message

Don't expect him to be able to read your mind. Formulate what you are trying to communicate into words, and tell him what is on your mind.

Don't send double messages. Your actions, facial expression, tone of voice, and body language all work together to communicate a message. If your words say one thing and your nonverbal communication says something else, there will be confusion.

2. Getting Through to Him

Be aware of his receptivity at a given moment. If you know he needs time after work to unwind, wait until he has shifted gears from work to home before trying to communicate.

Be aware of the emotional climate. If he is processing strong emotions that are dissimilar to the message you want to get across, try to find a time when his emotions are more in line with the tone of your message. However, also note that strong emotions such as anger may be used as defense mechanisms to keep from hearing something he may not want to hear. In situations where emotions flare whenever an important message becomes the topic of conversation, consider putting your message into writing and leaving it for him to receive. In this way the content will not be hampered by emotional defenses.

3. Listening

Don't interrupt. Listen to what he is saying, and keep listening until he is satisfied his message has been sent. You can respond with your comments once he is finished.

Maintain eye contact. Let him know you are with him by looking him in the eye as he talks (unless you are driving the car at the time!).

Don't focus your attention on preparing your reply or rebuttal while he is still talking. Focus on trying to clearly understand what he is saying and feeling.

Listen to the feelings beneath the words. Take note of his nonverbal cues. If the words don't match the body language, tone of voice, and facial expression, ask yourself what feelings might be beneath the words.

Don't assume anything! Once you have asked yourself what he might really mean and given yourself a plausible theory, don't assume your theory to be true. Instead, ask questions that will show if your theory is correct or not.

4. Giving and Receiving Feedback

Give nonverbal cues to let him know you are focused on him. A nod of the head, an empathetic smile, or a well-timed "uh-huh" can tell him that you are listening.

Reflect what you thought you heard him say, and ask if you understood him correctly. You will give him a chance to clarify his meaning.

Keep asking questions until what you think you heard is the same as what he was trying to get across. Ask questions beginning with phrases like, "Do I understand you to mean . . . ," "Are you trying to say . . . ," "Can you explain the part about . . . more clearly?"

When trying to send him a message, openly receive the feedback he gives you. Listen when he reflects what he thought he heard you say. Clarify your meaning. Answer his questions without allowing defensiveness to block communication.

PERSONAL EVALUATION

- Have you experienced frustration at times when it seemed you and your husband were approaching a conversation from two contrasting views of the world?
- Do you think your communication in marriage could be enriched by educating yourself about the differing communication styles used by men and women?
- Are you willing to learn and practice the skills that lead to good communication?

ACTION

Rate yourself on a scale of one to ten for how well you perform in the use of the four basic communication skills noted above (one is poor; five is average but could use improvement; ten is excellent).

Sending a clear message _____ Getting through to him _____ Listening _____ Giving and receiving feedback _____

Next, let your husband read this day's journey, and ask him to rate you on a scale of one to ten on the same four basic communication skills. Compare your scores. The chances are slim that your scores will be identical. Together practice the tips given for good communication until each clearly understands the other's rating of your communication skills. Remember the differing frames of reference, and discuss how they play into the quality of your communication.

REFLECTION

Consider how the ability to maintain good communication affects every aspect of married life. How could improving your ability to understand your mate and be understood by him enhance other facets of your marriage?

ENCOURAGEMENT

If you are willing to practice, you can master the skills that lead to good communication. When you polish these skills, you will benefit in your marriage, in other family relationships, in social settings, and in your work relationships.

FOOD FOR THOUGHT

The first duty of love is to listen.

—Paul Tillich

Be Considerate, Kind, and Affectionate

Little things can make a big difference in a marriage. It is not just what you do in day-to-day life but how you do it that will convey love to your husband. In general terms, the little niceties of life can be grouped in three categories: consideration, kindness, and affection. Each is not difficult to put into practice but will make a big difference in the life of the one being loved in this way.

Being considerate simply means that you regard him as a unique individual, with particular likes and dislikes, who has other influences to contend with in the course of life. The way you speak, prepare a sandwich, wear your hair, or fold the laundry can speak volumes of love when he realizes you chose to do it in the way he likes, being thoughtful of his preferences. Whenever you think about what he is going through at the moment and do something to anticipate his needs or feelings, you are being considerate of him. Some examples would be folding his socks the way he likes them instead of the way your mother taught you and putting whipped cream and sprinkles on his hot chocolate or a sprig of mint in his iced tea . . . if that is the way he likes it.

In his book *My Little Church Around the Corner*, Randolph Ray noted, "Kindness is the life's blood, the elixir of marriage. Kindness makes the difference between passion and caring. Kindness is tenderness.

Kindness is love. . . . Kindness is good will. Kindness says, 'I want to make you happy.' Kindness comes very close to the benevolence of God."

Kindness can become a good habit in your home. It is said that familiarity breeds contempt. There is danger in the everyday routines of marriage to allow familiarity to diminish the kindness you show your husband. You can be kind if you focus your attention in that direction. Being kind can be as simple as trying to be nice, being gentle and tender with him, and using good manners. It is an act of kindness to say "Please" and "Thank you" and "I'm sorry." You can choose to soften the rough spots, hold your tongue when tempted to throw out a snide remark, and give him the benefit of the doubt in questionable situations.

Being affectionate is a matter of displaying your love with a gentle touch. Giving him a warm hug, brushing your hand across his, bestowing an unexpected kiss, running your fingers through his hair, patting him on the back—these and hundreds of other small touches can display your genuine affection. If you find romance to be waning, start displaying nonsexual touches of affection (which may turn into presexual touches). They can get the sparks of romance going again.

PERSONAL EVALUATION

- What do you do in a special way just because you know your husband likes it that way?
- How do you show him kindness?
- What manners are used in your home and in relationship with your husband?

- Do you treat him with the same degree of kindness you would show a business associate or a guest?
- In the course of the day how many times would you guess you touch him affectionately?
- If you are not considerate, kind, and affectionate as a matter of practice, are you willing to begin practicing this way of relating?

ACTION

Focus your attention today on being considerate in the way you do things with and for him, practice being kind, and touch him affectionately. Don't tell him about the assignment. Take note of how different your behavior is from usual and what kind of response you get from him as you treat him this way.

REFLECTION

How did you feel about making these types of expressions of love? Awkward? Fearful of rejection? Loving? Happy with yourself? Do you believe that you must feel like being kind, considerate, and affectionate before you can be genuine in acting in these ways? When you began to act in these ways, did the feelings follow your actions?

ENCOURAGEMENT

Your choice to continually be considerate, kind, and affectionate will be rewarded by growing to feel more loving feelings for your husband and feel better about yourself.

FOOD FOR THOUGHT

I would like to have engraved inside every wedding band "Be kind to one another." This is the Golden Rule of marriage and the secret of making love last through the years.

—Randolph Ray

Practice Forgiveness

Laura couldn't believe what she was hearing. Her husband lowered his gaze to escape the dreadful look of shock, confusion, and outrage now consuming his wife's usually pleasant countenance. "I need you to forgive me," he stammered. "I don't want to tell you . . . but I can't go on living this lie. The affair is over now . . . and I'm so sorry . . . so terribly sorry. . . . But I couldn't go on pretending . . . deceiving you . . ." Laura's world was reeling. She had no idea. In the moments and hours that followed, she plummeted to the depths of despair, was struck with terrible fears, and was filled with rage. "I'll do anything to make things right again," he cried. "Can you ever forgive me?"

That was a very important question. A great wife must learn to practice forgiveness for two basic reasons: every man will need to be forgiven, and a woman who refuses to practice forgiveness will destroy her own well-being. No man or woman is perfect. In the course of life you and your husband will fail each other, sometimes in small ways, perhaps in major ways. Forgiveness brings reconciliation, displays love, and frees the heart of the one extending forgiveness from the stranglehold of bitterness. If you do not learn to understand and practice forgiveness, you cannot maintain a healthy marriage.

Misconceptions about forgiveness can convince you that forgiving your husband for some things is impossible. Let's deal with a few common misconceptions so you can begin practicing forgiveness.

Forgiveness does not require you to suppress or disguise your feelings generated by the offense. In Laura's case, she would spend many months processing her disturbing emotions wrought in the flames of his infidelity. Troubled feelings are valid even after you have chosen to forgive. Being forgiven does not excuse your husband from having to face the consequences of how his actions have affected you.

Forgiveness does not mean that you shield your husband from the natural consequences of what he has done. An extreme example of the danger of this misconception is seen in cases where wives are physically abused by their husbands and refuse to call the authorities for protection. A woman may say, "Well, I forgive him. I love him." She may not realize that she can forgive him and still stand back and allow the man to face his responsibility for the consequences of what he has done wrong.

Forgiveness is a choice you make over and over again. You may choose to forgive your husband today and tomorrow be tempted to take on the weight of wanting to make him pay. Tomorrow you can choose forgiveness again.

Forgiveness does not excuse wrong behavior. You may believe that if you forgive your husband, you will convey that what he did wrong was acceptable. Forgiveness pardons what you believe to be wrong; it does not mean you pretend that wrong is right.

Here is a view of forgiveness that may help you find a practical way to begin learning to forgive. In the Bible the visual picture of forgiveness is that of a list of offenses nailed to a cross with the blood of

Jesus "having wiped out the handwriting of requirements that was against us" (Col. 2:14). This description referred to the customary legal practice of listing the offenses for which the condemned person had been convicted. The list explained to anyone passing by why the person deserved to be punished. When the blood of the convict ran down over the list as he was dying, the death was accepted as having wiped out the handwriting of requirements held against him. Saying that Jesus gave forgiveness by having nailed our offenses to the cross shows that the prerequisite to forgiveness is that there is a list of offenses for which we have been convicted.

This image of being convicted before you can truly be forgiven and pardoned also applies to the process of forgiving others. You cannot truly forgive others until you have truly convicted them of all the requirements you have against them. When you list all the ways your husband hurt you, all the pain you experienced because (for whatever reasons) he failed to fulfill his responsibilities, you can take the list you have against him and leave it at the foot of the cross. You can acknowledge that what he did or failed to do was wrong and damaging (if it was), and that you choose to let go of your demands that he *pay* you back for the damage done. In this way you can acknowledge the value of your feelings, you can honestly deal with the debris in your life resulting from his sins, and you can proceed on your journey toward wholeness without getting bogged down with bitterness.

To truly forgive, you must not excuse the actual violations of what is right. To truly forgive, you must first convict the guilty party of every offense, then hand the list over to higher authorities. You can forgive and still hold him accountable, honestly acknowledging his responsibilities and allowing him to face the consequences of his failings. You just choose to transfer that weight off your shoulders.

Forgiveness involves letting go of your personal resentments and bitterness. One way to release them is to acknowledge and vent your true feelings rather than try to pretend that you feel fine. When you have been hurt, deceived, wronged, or betrayed, you don't feel fine. It will take time, but you can begin by determining to continue in the process until you experience the freedom that forgiveness gives you from the painful feelings associated with being hurt or betrayed.

PERSONAL EVALUATION

- Somewhere there is a list of all the offenses your husband has committed against you or those you love. Are you keeping account of every wrong suffered, adding it to a growing list in your head?
- Have you been pretending that he can do no wrong and overlooking the things he needs to be forgiven for because you hesitate to honestly recognize his failings?
- Did you stuff your true feelings that arose in reaction to some wrong on his part because you believed that if you truly forgave him, you would no longer be entitled to your feelings?
- Have you been able to take responsibility for your own life, regardless of how well or poorly your husband has behaved toward you?

ACTION

Today you will attempt to forgive your husband for the things you have against him in your heart. If you have already been practicing forgiveness, the list may be quite short. If you have never done this, you may have a long list, but you are probably familiar with what you have been holding against him. You are not looking for anything that is not there already.

Pretend that you are the one making out the same kind of legal statement of offenses referred to as being nailed to the cross. List your husband's failings. Include commitments he has broken, things he did that he shouldn't have done, and things he should have done but didn't.

For each one, acknowledge the validity of the pain caused in your life, and describe your feelings.

For each item, list the natural consequences. Recognize that forgiveness does not require you to protect him from these consequences.

Once you complete this list, check to see if you have added things you want to do to punish him that are not natural consequences of his behavior. Cross them off the list, and choose to give them up in your heart. Make a decision not to find ways to punish him for the wrongs he has done. Decide not to use past offenses as a weapon in future arguments.

Once you have emptied out all that you are holding against him, you can take the list before God and pray something like this:

Dear God,
    Here is the list of offenses that I have been holding against my husband. Thank You that You respect

our lives enough to recognize the need for account-ability for these kinds of hurtful acts and omissions. I don't want to hold on to them anymore. I will give them over to You and trust that You and he can work out any further arrangements. Amen!

REFLECTION

The issue of forgiveness is worthy of careful con-sideration. No one is perfect. Everyone needs forgive-ness from God and from others. Remember, the measurement that you use to judge your husband will be the very same measurement that will be used to measure your life. Don't let your life and marriage fall victim to unforgiveness.

ENCOURAGEMENT

You will need courage to forgive and lots of prac-tice, but forgiveness is something you can learn.

FOOD FOR THOUGHT

When you forgive somebody else you accept the re-sponsibility for your own future.

—Zig Ziglar

Confront Problems Honestly and Hopefully

A great wife doesn't pretend there are no problems; she confronts problems honestly and deals with them in positive ways. You have your problems, your husband has his problems, and you share problems. When you learn to face all problems with hope that they can be overcome, you will be a great help to your husband.

Every man needs someone to help him keep a realistic perspective. There will be times your husband will have problems he is trying to ignore or deny. You do him no favors by allowing him to live in a fantasy world. Denial can be deadly if the problems are allowed to compound. Whenever you are aware that your husband has a problem, even if he is in denial, you need to give him the gift of a loving confrontation. If you go along with his pretense, you will share the responsibility for whatever pain and destruction come. You cannot make him see the errors of his way, but you are responsible to honestly confront him and not spare him the consequences that result from untended problems in his life. If you pretend there isn't a problem and protect him from the consequences, he will have no personal motivation to deal with the problem.

You also will rely on your husband to help you see past your blind spots in recognizing and dealing with your problems. In marriage, a personal problem quickly can turn into a marriage problem. Your husband will experience the effects of problems in your life that are denied and neglected. He can give you support and encouragement in dealing with your problems, but you must make the ultimate decision to face them and get whatever help is necessary. When you learn to identify, face, and solve your personal problems, you will feel better about yourself, be less defensive in relationship with your husband, and be free to be your best.

One problem may make it extremely difficult to deal with all other problems of a personal nature. That is the problem of unhealthy shame. Unhealthy shame is the deeply rooted belief that you are a flawed human being, that there is something wrong with you that can't be changed and must be hidden. When unhealthy shame is at the foundation of your self-image, you avoid, hide, or run from all problems because you don't believe there is a solution. Rather, you see problems as evidence of your flawed nature and fear being exposed and rejected. If you think your issues may be related to unhealthy shame, get help coping with them before trying to focus on other problems. Once you are free from the grip of unhealthy shame, you will have the hope necessary to face and resolve your personal problems.

PERSONAL EVALUATION

- Are you able to deal with problems honestly with the hope that any problem can be solved?
- Have you learned good problem-solving skills?
- If not, are you willing to educate yourself and learn the process for solving problems?
- Do you ignore your husband's problems and

shield him from the natural consequences resulting from untended personal problems? Why
do you do this?

ACTION

List five of your personal problems.

List five of your husband's personal problems.

List five problems you and your husband share.

Next to each one, place a *C* if the problem is being
confronted and dealt with in some positive way;
place a *D* if the problem is being denied by someone
and write the name of who is in denial; place a question mark if the problem is recognized but you and
your husband are not sure what to do about it, so you
are doing nothing.

Plan some time to talk with your husband about
how both of you can learn to deal with the problems
in your lives. Ask him to tell you which of your personal problems concern him most. Listen to see if he
may be able to see problems in your life that you may
need to face and deal with. Tell him about the problems you see in his life that concern you, and offer to
help him resolve them if there is anything you can
do.

Choose one of your personal problems that needs
attention and work on finding a solution. Once you
have that one solved, go back to the list and tackle
another one.

REFLECTION

How do you feel dealing with problems? Do you
have confidence that you can find a solution? Think
of all the problems you have successfully solved in

your lifetime. What were the common processes involved?

ENCOURAGEMENT

You can solve your problems if you are willing to face them honestly and get the help you need.

FOOD FOR THOUGHT

What counts in making a happy marriage is not so much how compatible you are but how you deal with incompatibility.

—George Levinger

Acknowledge His Sacrifices

Her name really is Fortune. When asked about the origin of such an unusual first name, she explained, "My father says he always dreamed of making a fortune. When he chose to marry and raise a family, he realized that I may be the only fortune he will ever make." Fortune's father willingly made a choice for the fortune of his family over the other kinds of fortune he might have given his life to pursue. That devotion deserves to be recognized.

In the movie *It's a Wonderful Life*, the lead character George Bailey makes a series of sacrifices out of love for his family. When he was a young man, he had high hopes of seeing the world. As the years slip by, he sees other men leave the small town where he lives to seek fame and fortune. He stays behind, choosing the steady path of love and devotion to his parents, wife, and children. He occupies a rather mundane job at the thrift and loan, while his dreams are consumed on the sacrificial altar of love for his family. He begins to doubt the value of his life, wonders at the worth of the sacrifices he has chosen to make, and experiences the despair known to men who find themselves locked into jobs and life-styles that are far less than what they once dreamed of for themselves.

Every man wants to believe that his life makes a difference in this world. In *It's a Wonderful Life*, George gets to see the value of his life and sacrifices with the help of an angel. In real life, you may be the only one who can help your husband see the value of his sacrifices and how he has chosen to spend his life. You can do that only if you notice his sacrifices and consider the value of what your husband does for his family.

With every choice your husband made, he also chose to give up something else. When he chose to marry, he gave up a degree of freedom. When children came along and he chose to provide for them, he might have passed up opportunities that would not provide his family the security they needed. He made the choices willingly, but he experienced a loss nonetheless. There may be seasons of doubt when he reflects on the choices he made and wonders how life might have been different if he had not had the responsibilities of a wife and family. He may experience the loss of his dreams as he grows older and does not accomplish the things he hoped to do. A great wife will be sensitive to the sacrifices made by her husband and appreciate the loss involved.

Here are some things you can do to show appreciation for the sacrifices he is making:

- Tell him how much you appreciate what he does for you.
- Mention how much his hard work means to you.
- Take note of the benefits you receive as the result of what he does with his time, energy, and money.
- When he is required to do something for work that inconveniences you, consider whether what he is doing is one way he expresses his love for you and your children. Be understanding and supportive rather than act as though he were showing you a lack of love.

PERSONAL EVALUATION

- What has your husband given up for the sake of your family?
- When he works long hours, taking him away from you, is he doing it as an expression of love for you?
- What dreams has he seen slip away as life progressed and he accepted the responsibilities of being a husband and father?

ACTION

Ask your husband to talk to you about what he has sacrificed for you and your family. Ask him to tell you the dreams he once had that may be slipping away from him. Think about what he says, and compile a list of how his sacrifices benefit you and your family. Compose this list into a thank-you note expressing appreciation for the sacrifices. Try to specify how the sacrifices he has made are valuable, how they will pay off in your life and the life of your family.

Remember to end the Widow Game today and list everything you appreciate about your husband.

REFLECTION

What feelings did you experience as you listened to him talk about his sacrifices? What feelings did he seem to be experiencing? What does the value of what he has given up for you say about the value of his love?

How have your feelings changed by playing the Widow Game for the past week? How does your new perspective toward your husband motivate you to show him your love and appreciation?

ENCOURAGEMENT

Your appreciation of his sacrifices can help define the value and meaning of his life. That is a precious gift to any man.

FOOD FOR THOUGHT

Self-sacrifice is one of the most beautiful displays of love anyone can witness.

Give Yourself (and Him) Some Time

Being a great wife takes more than desire; it also takes time. You can't be a great wife if you don't take time to nourish and refresh yourself in ways that allow you to be your best, time to love your husband, and time to learn new things and practice the skills that will make you a great partner over the course of life. You also need to give yourself time in terms of being patient with yourself. Don't demand overnight success with the changes you want to make. Changing habit patterns and life-style is not usually easy or instantaneous.

Now is the time in your journey to rethink the distribution of time under your control. Since you probably don't have much spare time, you will need to eliminate some activities that are unnecessary or less important than your newly focused priorities. You must choose to take time and weave your good intentions into your daily life.

PERSONAL EVALUATION

- Does your current schedule reflect the time you want to spend being your best, loving your husband, and partnering with him in life?
- Are there commitments you have taken on yourself, which interfere with being a great wife, that could be delegated to others?

- Are you willing to make some scheduling changes to enhance your marriage and allow yourself the time it takes to be a great wife?

ACTION

Chronicle your twenty-four-hour days for what you have planned for the next two weeks. Your goal is to mold your real schedule to fit the shape of your true values.

Step One

Sketch out a diagram that depicts twenty-four hours for each day in the coming two weeks (if you already keep a calendar, refer to the plans you have recorded for the next two weeks).

Step Two

Fill in the hours that you regularly spend sleeping, eating, grooming, and taking care of other physical necessities.

Step Three

Fill in the hours that are already committed to ongoing activities that you are not in a position to change, such as school, work, church, and so on.

Step Four

Fill in all of the appointments you have planned for the next two weeks, such as going to the dentist or attending meetings, sporting events, social events, and so on.

Anything left open on your calendar should represent areas of opportunity: opportunities to work at being your best, to love your husband, and to move in the direction of being a better life partner.

Step Five

Make a list of the things you would like to do that fit into the three categories of being a great wife.

Step Six

Schedule at least one hour daily for taking care of yourself in the particular ways you have chosen. Schedule specific times each day for showing love to your husband in some of the ways you have chosen. Arrange with your husband to schedule a date for one evening each week. Schedule time each week for working on developing the knowledge and skills you will soon identify for your long-term goals of being a great partner with your husband. (Even though you have yet to focus on these long-range goals, you can make time for them now.)

Step Seven

Look at the list of things you chose to do in Step Five and *schedule them into your daily calendar as appointments*. If they do not fit into appointed times, *commit them to a specific day*, such as Thursday afternoon or evening.

This commitment should be realistic, or you will become discouraged. A small improvement that is within reach is better than an idealistic calendar that will prove overwhelming.

REFLECTION

Are you excited about whatever changes you are able to make in the right direction, or are you feeling somewhat guilty that you can't do more?

ENCOURAGEMENT

Remember, changing your schedule is a major undertaking. Committing yourself to and following through on positive changes will make a positive difference as you repeat them over the course of days, months, and years.

FOOD FOR THOUGHT

With the high value placed on time, when you give your husband the time of day, you are showing how valuable your relationship with him truly is.

Characteristics of a Great Partner

Marriage is much more than a relationship of love; it is also a partnership for life. Consider this poem by Robert Frost that became the inscription on the gravestone above the grave where he and his wife, Elinor, were buried:

> Two such as you with such a master speed,
> Cannot be parted nor be swept away
> From one another once you are agreed
> That life is only life forevermore
> Together wing to wing and oar to oar.

What a beautiful monument to their lifetime partnership! Within these verses are some clues to how you can be a great partner in life with your husband. Let's start with them and continue looking at other things you can do to make the most of your lifetime partnership.

Agree in your heart that life together is life forevermore. Don't allow yourself to see your commitment in marriage as anything less than love for a lifetime.

Fly wing to wing. Face the changing winds of life together, heading in the same direction. Don't turn against each other.

Agree on common purposes and goals. Once you know your shared purposes and goals in any area of life, you can make independent decisions that will further your common aim.

Major on your strengths, and allow your husband to major on his. Each of you has particular strong points and points of weakness. Work together to find ways that each person's strengths are used to the maximum good of both.

Complement him at his points of weakness. Instead of tearing him down where he is weak, look to see what you can do to support him and lift him up until he can grow stronger in areas of weakness. If there is some area where he is weak and you are strong, design your functions within the relationship so that you cover the area. He can do the same for you in your areas of weakness.

Respect the position your husband holds, of being accountable before God for the care of his family. You are an equal partner with a differing role to play. As a great partner, you will respect yourself and willingly lend your support to your husband as he oversees family matters. Support him; don't try to supplant him.

Agree to disagree. When you agree on the major issues of your shared purposes and goals, you can agree to disagree on minor points or areas where you have differing views.

Clearly communicate your expectations.

Share your wisdom with him. Your husband needs your perspective and input on all decisions affecting your family. Share what you know, your sensitivity to certain situations, your perceptions and opinions.

Never forget that you are on the same team. When you keep this fact in mind, you will not seek to tear him down or compete against him.

PERSONAL EVALUATION

- How do you feel about having a structure of authority within the family? Have you experienced the abuse of authority by men, which causes you to feel uncomfortable with respecting your husband's position of leadership in the family?
- What other characteristics for a great partner can you think of?

ACTION

Reread the list above, and think of examples for each point where you have displayed that particular characteristic of a great partner.

List things you feel you need to do or characteristics you need to develop to become a great life partner.

Write a description of the shared purpose for your life together with your husband. You may want to discuss it with him if you are not already clear about it.

List the specific goals you and your husband share in the various areas of life where you partner together: in your sexual relationship, in finances, in home and family, in spirituality, and in any other ways you can think of.

REFLECTION

When both you and your husband have passed away, what would you want to be said as the epitaph of your lifelong marriage?

When you think about marriage lasting a lifetime,

do you have reasons to fear that yours may not last that long? What can you do to change things so those fears become unfounded?

ENCOURAGEMENT

We often focus on the marriages that don't make it as lifetime partnerships. But plenty of marriages do last a lifetime. Yours can be one of them.

FOOD FOR THOUGHT

To keep the fire burning brightly there's one easy rule: keep the two logs together, near enough to keep each other warm and far enough apart—about a finger's breadth—for breathing room. Good fire, good marriage—same rule.

—Marnie Reed Crowell

Being a Great Sexual Partner

Since you and your husband have made the commitment to keep yourselves exclusively for each other as sexual partners, being a great sexual partner is important. That is not to say you should do anything you are not comfortable with. That is to say sexuality is a significant part of your being, and sex within marriage needs to be nurtured.

Here are some ways you can be a great sexual partner:

Take care of your self-esteem. When you are feeling good about yourself, you will be much more comfortable with sexual intimacy. Sex within marriage is intended to be a knowing of each other. If you feel bad about yourself, you won't have a desire to be known. Get help for any problems that keep you from intimacy with your husband.

Get to know what you like, and let your husband know. He can't read your mind. Tell him when he does something that gives you pleasure. Tell him the things you would like to try. If he is doing things that you don't like, talk about it. Learning to communicate your sexual needs and desires is basic to a healthy relationship.

Get to know what he likes, and be generous in pleasing him. Ask him what he likes; notice his responses; become a student of what he enjoys.

Get enough rest. You can't be a great sexual partner when you are exhausted. Taking care to get enough rest is a way of preparing to make love to your husband.

Plan time for intimacy. Don't just expect great sex to happen. Plan time for it, then guard your time together.

Be creative. Don't let sex become routine. Think of ways you can make sex new. Change your surroundings; change your bedroom attire; change locations.

Educate yourself. You can learn to be a great sexual partner. Read books, magazine articles, and other materials that will help you educate yourself about human sexuality.

Get help for problems that interfere with a satisfying sex life. If you are experiencing problems that you don't know how to solve on your own, consider seeing a therapist who could help you identify the factors contributing to your lack of sexual satisfaction and deal with them. Excellent help is available. There is no reason for you to be deprived of sexual satisfaction in marriage when you can find help.

Considering being a great sexual partner can touch on very sensitive issues. How you feel about yourself sexually is at the heart of who you are. That can be especially painful if your husband has expressed disappointment with you as a sexual partner or he has used your "inability to satisfy" him as an excuse for his flirtations or infidelities. If your husband has allowed himself to become sexually involved with someone else or is struggling with lust for other women, he may try to convince you the fault lies with you. Don't believe it. These types of struggles and behaviors say much more about him than they say about you.

PERSONAL EVALUATION

- Have you ever told your husband specifically what you enjoy sexually?
- Are you sure you know what he enjoys?
- What have you done to educate yourself about sexual enjoyment in marriage?
- What problems do you have that interfere with sexual intimacy? What are you doing to resolve them?

ACTION

Go to the library or bookstore, and get a book to educate you on ways you could enrich your sex life.

Plan an evening or a weekend alone with your husband when you can discuss how each of you feels about your sexual relationship, share what you would like to see happen to enrich your sexual relationship, and listen to what your husband has to say.

Check your calendar, which you recently rescheduled, to make sure you planned enough time to rest and to enjoy your husband intimately.

REFLECTION

Fantasize about a wonderful sexually satisfying encounter with your husband. Focus on how he would please you and how you would please him.

ENCOURAGEMENT

Giving attention to yourself as a sexual partner can bring new life to your routine married life.

FOOD FOR THOUGHT

Meaningful touching outside the bedroom can light sparks in a marriage, and meaningful communication can fan the flames.

—Gary Smalley

Being a Great Partner in Building Home and Family

Building a home and family is at the heart of what life is all about. Home and family are more than arrangements of things and people. These forces shape the lives of those you hold most dear. The kind of partner you are in building a home and raising your children will have a tremendous impact on our world.

Consider these words of Barbara Bush when she addressed a graduating class:

> Cherish your human connections: your relationships with friends and family. For several years, you've had impressed upon you the importance to your career of dedication and hard work. This is true, but as important as your obligations as a doctor, lawyer, or business leader will be, you are a human being first and those human connections—with spouses, with children, with friends—are the most important investments you will ever make.

> At the end of your life, you will never regret not having passed one more test, not winning one more verdict or not closing one more deal. You will regret time not spent with a husband, a friend, a child or a parent.

> Whatever the era . . . whatever the times, one thing will never change: Fathers and mothers, if you have

children . . . they must come first. You must read to your children, you must hug your children, you must love your children.

Your success as a family . . . our success as a society . . . depends *not* on what happens at the White House, but on what happens inside your house.

Your role as a partner in building your home and family is vital. Today you will consider what you do and some things you could do to become better at partnering with your husband in this area.

PERSONAL EVALUATION

- What do you do to build the success of your home and family?
- Do you feel that you are in partnership with your husband to build home and family, or do you feel alone in these responsibilities?
- In what respects do you feel that you are bearing responsibilities for home and family alone when you would like to have more of your husband's support?
- What talents and abilities are you using creatively to build home and family?
- What areas of knowledge or ability do you feel you lack that keep you from building your home and family the way you would like?
- If you could have outside help with some of the work of managing your home, where would you say you need the most assistance?

ACTION

Write a letter to yourself about how your success as a family and our success as a society are positively influenced by what you do each day in your home.

Consider the areas where you would like to improve your ability to build your home and family. Then list three things you could learn about that would help you increase your knowledge of managing your home. List three things you could do to develop the skills needed to build up your home and family.

Set one long-range goal to improve your ability to be a great partner in building a home and family. Write it down; plan how you could achieve it.

REFLECTION

Take a few moments to consider Barbara Bush's words, and think about the greater value of the things you do each day.

ENCOURAGEMENT

Being a great wife is one of the foundations of a successful home and family. Your efforts have far-reaching effects.

FOOD FOR THOUGHT

When two people love each other, they don't look at each other, they look in the same direction.
—Ginger Rogers

Being a Great Spiritual Partner

Human beings are made in the image of God—body, mind, and spirit. When you enter into the union of marriage, there is a spiritual union as well as a physical one. It is understandable to want to share your spiritual dimension and your comprehension of spiritual things with your husband. Sharing a common faith in God and similar spiritual experiences can be a very rich part of your marriage. When you and your husband do not share a common faith or spiritual understanding, there can be added tension in the relationship. Whatever your particular situation, here are some guidelines to help you consider how you can be a great spiritual partner within your marriage:

Seek God. Draw close to God, and allow your relationship with God to enrich your life. Develop the qualities of true spirituality: humility, love, generosity, faith, courage, strength, and serenity.

Allow the richness of what your spiritual life brings to you to overflow in love for your husband.

Pray for your husband. Regardless of your husband's spiritual experience, you are always free to pray for him. Pray for his well-being, his job, his health, blessings in his life. Pray about everything that concerns him.

Sincerely seek to understand what he believes and why. Try to understand the influences that have shaped his spiritual experience.

Never allow yourself to become self-righteous or

condescending toward him if he doesn't share your beliefs or spiritual experience.

PERSONAL EVALUATION

- How would you describe the spiritual aspect of your life?
- How do your beliefs about God affect your family relationships?
- Do you know what your husband believes and what influences have shaped those beliefs?
- What can you do with your husband that might enrich your lives spiritually?

ACTION

Pray for your own spiritual enrichment. Pray for your husband. Pray for God's help to become the best wife you can possibly be.

If you are not accustomed to praying, don't worry. Just talk to God as though He were a friend sitting with you and wanting to know what is on your heart and mind. If you prefer, you can write your prayer in the form of a letter to God.

REFLECTION

What are you hungry for spiritually? Are you experiencing a desire for a greater sense of meaning in your life? Consider how you and your husband could partner together to enrich your spiritual lives.

ENCOURAGEMENT

Seek God. The Bible promises that everyone who seeks God with a sincere heart will find Him. When you do, whether it's for the first time or for a fresh touch of His hand, your life will be enriched.

FOOD FOR THOUGHT

God says, "And you will seek Me and find Me, when you search for Me with all your heart."
—Jeremiah 29:13

Being a Great Economic Partner

Work and money play a central role in the way you live your life. They are also often at the center of marital conflict. In marriage, you are an economic partner with your husband. In the book *Partners in Love*, Alanson B. Houghton had this to say: "Money is so central to our daily economic and emotional well-being that partners, especially marriage partners, must understand its dynamics and how the other feels about money."

In our society, the changing economic climate is having a tremendous impact on marriage and the family. Most women work outside the home as well as bear the major share of work within the home caring for the needs of their husbands and children. Being able to juggle these responsibilities while balancing your life and nurturing your marriage is no easy task. Whether you work outside your home in a fulfilling career of your choosing or you work in a job that you don't particularly relish as a matter of financial necessity, you will still face the struggles of trying to keep your priorities in order, dealing with uncertainty over what is best for your children, and perhaps handling stress that comes from your husband's insecurity about his identity now that he is no longer the sole breadwinner, especially if your income is higher than his.

Whatever your economic circumstances, there are trade-offs that will test your confidence in your choices regarding where your time and energy are being expended during your children's early years. Many experts in the field of child development agree that children need their mother's care without substitute for the first six months of life, and they strongly recommend the children be home with one primary caregiver (preferably their mother) for the first three years. If you work outside the home, you may face tremendous guilt and self-doubt. If you stay home with your children, you may feel out of step with your peers. If you and your husband are not in agreement about where you are working, and whether or not you are home to care for the children, you will experience added pressures. In these economic realities of life, you and your husband must work out shared priorities and goals, helping each other do the best you can to care for your children.

Another thing to consider is whether you allow the work of caring for your children and the work outside the home to take precedence over your relationship with your husband. Dr. Joyce Brothers has this to say in her book *What Every Woman Ought to Know About Love and Marriage:*

> It is time to face up to the chief threat to your marriage—forgetting or neglecting to put your husband first. There are so many demands on your time and energy that it is usually the squeaky wheels that get the grease. And the squeakiest wheels are the child and the job. You tell yourself that your husband understands the pressures on you. He probably does. He will also understand that you are putting your job and child ahead of him. . . . Don't let yourself fall into this trap. Make sure he knows he is first.

Today you will consider things you can do to be a great economic partner. Here are some examples:

Discuss, clarify, and agree on family priorities related to finances, child care, and distribution of labor within your family. Your children are your and your husband's responsibility. Between the two of you, figure out a way to care for them according to their needs.

Check yourself to make sure you are keeping your relationship with your husband first in priority. If you never have time or energy to devote to loving him, your declaration that he is first will ring hollow.

Plan for the future together with your husband regarding the work of life. Each of you has aspirations and concerns about what you want to accomplish and achieve. Take time to communicate about what he wants his life's work to be and what you want your life's work to be. Help him plan for a future that moves toward the kind of work he wants to do, and ask for his help in doing the same.

Respect your own value and the value of the work you do. Regardless of whether you are being paid wages or how your wages compare to your husband's wages, your work is important.

Discuss and agree on financial goals for spending, earnings, saving, investing, and budgeting.

Be financially informed and responsible even if your husband takes primary care of family finances. Know your budget, your net worth, information regarding insurance policies, investments, and the like. Make sure you have a current will. Think through financial decisions with your husband.

Educate yourself in areas of finance and economics where you lack understanding.

Do your best to make your financial resources go as far as possible. Learn to make the most of your money by reducing your debts, spending wisely, and learning to live in ways that do not waste the money you have at your disposal.

PERSONAL EVALUATION

- Have you and your husband agreed on priorities for child care, work outside the home for each of you, and time together?
- Do you understand how your husband feels about money, you working outside the home or staying home to care for your children, and the economic changes taking place in our society?
- Is he feeling threatened by the changing societal roles?
- Do you feel confident as a partner in the economic area of life with your husband?
- Are you financially informed and responsible as a partner in family finances?
- Do you have a will?
- What problems in your marriage relate to financial or work-related matters?
- Can you see how becoming better informed and educated on economic matters could strengthen your marriage partnership?
- What are some specific areas where you could improve in economic matters?
- Are you willing to take steps to become better educated?

ACTION

Cite one area of conflict related to economics. Consider what you could do to become a better economic partner that would help resolve the conflict.

Set a specific goal to learn something new that would help you deal with the issues related to the problem.

Set a goal of what you can do in the next six months to help resolve this conflict by being a better economic partner.

If you and your family are not clearly agreed on your family priorities related to work and child care, discuss these issues and set your priorities together.

REFLECTION

How do your feelings about work and money affect your marriage?

ENCOURAGEMENT

You can learn the things you need to know to be a great economic partner. Having your finances in order will help your home be in order.

FOOD FOR THOUGHT

Life is work, and everything you do is so much more experience. Sometimes you work for wages, sometimes not, but what does anybody make but a living? And whatever you have you must use or lose.

—Henry Ford

Extending and Diversifying Your Network of Support

It is easy to fall into the habit of relying heavily on your husband, even to the point of weighing him down with many of your needs that others could just as easily meet. As discussed on Day 6, a great wife will take responsibility for her own life. You have been doing that in the process of completing this journey. Part of taking responsibility for your life involves developing a strong network of support to help meet your needs, which extends far beyond your husband and one or two others.

Today you will look for ways of extending your network of support so that you will not be a mountain of neediness whenever your husband looks at you. You will still rely on your husband to be a support to you, but you will also diversify so that you are not utterly dependent on him.

Here are some times and situations when it might be best to have someone other than your husband fill a particular need for you:

You may expect your husband to help you in ways he is not equipped to help. Others may have more skill or knowledge in a particular area, and they could be of greater help in that way.

You may demand that your husband meet a need you think only he can fulfill, for example, making you feel more feminine. In reality, although your husband's response to you may make you feel more feminine, you can do many things for yourself to validate your feminine feelings.

You may expect your husband to help you in ways that he could do, but others could do just as well. A better idea may be to hire someone to help with time-consuming mundane tasks while you and your husband take the time to be together.

PERSONAL EVALUATION

- Who were the people and organizations you depended on in the exercise for Day 6?
- What needs did you list on Day 6 for which you depended primarily on your husband to help you meet them?
- What have you decided you need to do, learn, or pursue to become the kind of wife you want to be?
- What kind of help will you need to support you as you pursue being a great wife in the ways you have selected?

ACTION

List each need from the personal evaluation above. For each one you originally noted on Day 6, you already indicated where you turn for support; find two additional sources of help and/or support—other than your husband—to supplement them. (You may be thinking there are some needs, particularly sexual needs, that you shouldn't take to anyone other than your husband. However, even when dealing with sexual needs, you can turn to sources of support, counseling, and knowledge that speak to the needs at a heart level.) For each need you have added to your list in response to taking this journey, look for two sources of help and/or support as well.

You are going to learn how to track down new resources of help and encouragement you can build into your life support network. To help you with this task, here is some information on how to identify resources in general terms. It should get you headed in the right direction so that you can add to your network of support.

Tremendous resources are available for every imaginable facet of marriage and life. Once you have identified specific goals and objectives, it becomes fairly easy to find resources to give you the knowledge you need, help you develop the skills you want, and provide practical assistance and support. Listing many specific resources would not be beneficial since each person taking the journey is focused on her own goals. I want to give you some ideas about how to track down the resources you need.

You probably have access to more resources than you could ever exhaust just working through your local library and your telephone directory. Here are the steps to finding resources in any area of interest:

Step One

Identify the area where you need help or more information. (You have already done this.)

Step Two

Check at your local library for books on the topic or related topics. You can go to the card catalog (a file of cards that represents every book available through the library). The cards are listed by topic and by author's last name. Most libraries have a wide variety of books on family and marriage-related issues. Or ask a librarian to recommend some books on the topic or guide you to the section of the library that holds the books you need.

Step Three

Contact organizations that are set up to deal with issues related to your area of interest. A great resource for any family-related issue is Focus on the Family. You can call them and receive leads about almost any conceivable family issue. The telephone number is 719-531-3400.

- Another way to track down groups and organizations is to use your telephone directory. Look under city, county, state, and federal governments for numbers of agencies. If you are not sure that a particular agency can help you, call and explain what information or help you are trying to locate. Staff persons will usually know where to direct you if they cannot help you.
- A growing network of treatment centers and recovery groups has resources available. You can contact counseling offices, treatment centers, or universities and usually get leads about people, groups, and organizations that help individuals in specific ways.
- You can call the offices of radio talk shows that deal with issues related to your area of interest. Radio talk programs have to keep an extensive listing of guests who address various topics. They will probably have a list of referrals to groups and organizations as well.
- The best resources are human resources. Within

your community, there are church groups, women's groups, recovery groups, parenting groups, educational seminars, and so on. To tap into these meetings, you can contact your local Chamber of Commerce.

- Develop and nurture friendships with other women. If you are still waiting for your husband to fill your emotional needs in the same way your high-school girlfriend did, give it up. Some needs can be filled only through friendships with women.

The real key to finding information and resources is to keep on seeking, keep on asking, and keep on knocking. Once you know what you want to accomplish, what tasks you need to complete to reach your goals, what information or help you lack, it's just a matter of persistent effort to track down the resources. Use these tips to find at least two additional sources of help to meet your needs.

REFLECTION

How do you feel about reaching out to others and extending your network of support beyond your previous limits?

ENCOURAGEMENT

Reaching out and making new connections with people can be intimidating. Remember, when you have a wide network of support, you will be better able to give of yourself to your husband without always coming across to him as desperately needy.

FOOD FOR THOUGHT

Ask, and it will be given to you; seek, and you will find; knock, and it will be opened to you. For everyone who asks receives, and he who seeks finds, and to him who knocks it will be opened.

—Jesus Christ

Continuing to Be a Great Wife

Being a great wife means balancing your resources and abilities in each of three areas: being your best, knowing and loving your husband, and being a great partner with him in life. As you continue to keep this healthy balance, you can live with the confidence that you are being a great wife.

You have already taken decisive action to learn new things about each area. You have a notebook with short-term and long-term goals for each area. Why stop now? Each time you achieve one of your goals in each area, choose another to replace it. In this way you will continue to grow and find a sense of confidence that comes from knowing you are continuing to move in the right direction.

Your journey continues throughout your life. The important thing in staying a great wife is not losing momentum. Each day, one day at a time, keep your dreams clearly in sight, goals well defined, tasks identified, obstacles targeted for attack, and your relationship with your husband well nourished. The only way to do that is to plan and guard time for reflection.

Your life is divided into days, weeks, months, and years. At each of these segments of life, you can ensure being a great wife by planning time for reviewing your life and revising your choices. To stay current with the changes life brings and continue being a great wife, plan for the following:

Daily Quiet Time

Give yourself some time and space to reflect on your life each day. Pray for wisdom and strength. Read nourishing materials. Think about what you are facing and how you can best face the challenges of the day without compromising your priorities in life. Refresh your positive attitude. Give thanks for all that you have, your health, your family, the opportunities for growth.

Weekly Rest and Reflection

One day each week, relieve yourself of the burden of work, and refresh yourself. Take this time to enjoy relationship with your family, play together, worship God together, and enjoy one another's company. On your weekly day of rest, consider how you did the previous week in your role as a wife; consider what the week held for your husband and what he might need from you in the coming week. During your weekly checkup, examine how well you are nourishing yourself so that you can be your best, how well you are loving your husband and partnering with him in facing what life has brought that week. You can take note of where you may be getting out of balance and make corrections before major problems have time to develop.

Your weekly self-checkup should include considering how much quality time you have shared with your husband that week. Dr. Charlie Shedd recommends at least fifteen minutes of heart-to-heart conversation between husband and wife each day. That is, you discuss what is going on inside your heart, mind, and emotions rather than just the incidentals of life. He also recommends a weekly night out together to enjoy each other. At the end of each week, take note of whether you have made room for your daily heart-to-heart chats and your weekly date.

Monthly Enrichment

Plan caring for yourself as a wife into your monthly calendar. As you do whatever form of planning you do for each coming month, plan ways to enrich your marriage. Having a weekend away with your husband can be a romantic boost to your marriage. But these marriage enrichment times will not happen by accident. You have to plan for them.

Yearly Reviews

In the week between Christmas and New Year's Eve, take time to review your goals for life. Keep a notebook with all your goals in writing: family goals, financial goals, social goals, educational goals, spiritual goals, career goals, and so on. What goals have you accomplished in the past year? Revise your written goals for each area by listing immediate changes you want to make, short-term goals (under six months), one-year goals, five-year goals, and twenty-five-year goals. You will be amazed at how writing your goals down and reviewing them on an annual basis can keep you from growing stagnant. Including your goals for being a great wife will keep your marriage from growing stagnant, too.

PERSONAL EVALUATION

- After taking your journey, do you have a sense of balance in all three areas? Are you taking clearly defined steps and making commitments to achieve balance in all three areas? Are you ready to see yourself as a great wife?

- Do you currently take daily quiet time, a weekly day of rest, times to plan your monthly calendar, and annual times for revising your old goals and setting new ones?
- If not, can you see the value in doing so enough to motivate yourself to make these changes?

ACTION

Decide if you will continue to use your personal growth notebook to record and monitor your progress on the goals you set in terms of being your best, knowing and loving your husband, and partnering with him in life.

Forgive yourself for whatever you might have felt guilty for in the past in terms of being a great wife, and make a commitment to continue moving forward and making positive choices to overcome whatever obstacles present themselves along the road of life.

Take your quiet time today.

REFLECTION

How does taking charge of planning time for reflection, reviews, and revisions help you gain confidence that you are being a great wife?

ENCOURAGEMENT

Your willingness to weave your good intentions into the fabric of your days, weeks, months, and years will bring your desire to be a great wife into reality.

FOOD FOR THOUGHT

The art of progress is to preserve order amid change
and to preserve change amid order.
—Alfred North Whitehead

Give Yourself Credit and Decide Where You Go From Here

Although you have come to the end of the 30-day journey outlined in this book, your personal journey continues. Being a great wife is a continuing goal. I hope you have come to recognize that you are able to be a great wife when you choose to be. Sure, you might have identified some areas that need continued attention, but every human relationship requires ongoing care.

PERSONAL EVALUATION

Today, give yourself the credit due you. In the commitment you signed at the beginning of this journey, you promised, "I will not focus my attention on how far I fall short of being the ideal wife. I will focus my attention on *moving forward* from where I am today toward what I want to be." By participating in each day's journey, you have taken many steps toward being a great wife. Don't take them for granted. Take time to see the changes, and appreciate what you have done to reach your desired goal.

ACTION

Look back at Days 6 through 21. Each one focused attention on ways you could make immediate changes that would contribute to being a great wife.

Consider all the small changes you have made. They all make a difference. Look at the topic for each day and list at least one specific thing you did to move in that direction: What did you do to . . .

. . . accept responsibility for your life?
. . . appreciate what you have to offer?
. . . take care of your health and appearance?
. . . set boundaries of self-respect?
. . . choose to go beyond his expectations?
. . . renew your wholehearted commitment?
. . . dump the man of your dreams and accept the real man you married?
. . . create a sensational atmosphere?
. . . display respect for him and his work?
. . . appreciate him?
. . . water the seeds of greatness within him?
. . . practice good communication skills?
. . . be considerate, kind, and affectionate?
. . . practice forgiveness?
. . . confront problems honestly and hopefully?
. . . acknowledge his sacrifices?

In Days 22 through 28, you focused your attention on areas relating to more long-range goals. Look at each area; note at least one thing you are great at in being a great partner in life.

- What personal qualities are your strengths in making you a great partner for life?
- What is one thing you have done to move toward being a great sexual partner?
- What is one thing you have done to move toward being a great partner in building a home and family?

- What is one thing you have done to move toward being a great spiritual partner?
- What is one thing you have done to move toward being a great economic partner?
- What is one thing you have done to extend and diversify your network of support?

Don't overlook your progress! Applaud yourself for the progress you have made and for the awareness you have developed in terms of where you need to progress further. It takes courage to recognize areas of weakness and choose to get help to strengthen you in ways that will help you be a great wife. Next, you will take stock of the areas where you have had the courage to see needed changes and commit yourself to seeking change.

- In what area do you need to make the most progress in terms of being your best?
- In what area do you need to make the most progress in terms of knowing and/or loving your husband?
- In what area do you need to make the most progress in terms of being a greater partner in life?

Choose to end this journey by turning these issues you recognize as areas of potential growth into specific goals for your future.

Give yourself a reward for your progress. One of the best rewards you could give yourself would be to acknowledge that you are a great wife and getting better all the time. If your husband has taken note of your sincere efforts and progress, let him help you celebrate your success.

REFLECTION

Remember that on Day 2 you had your husband write his definition of what it means to be a great wife? Now is the time to read it. Read his definition and decide if you fill the bill of what he described. Consider whether you surpass it or whether you disagree with his definition. Read over your original definition written on Day 2. How has your definition changed in the process of taking this journey?

ENCOURAGEMENT

If you have completed each day of this journey, you have displayed tremendous effort and love for yourself and your husband. Your efforts will be rewarded.

FOOD FOR THOUGHT

We cannot do everything at once, but we can do something at once.

—Calvin Coolidge

Sometimes problems are too difficult to handle alone on a 30-day journey. If you feel that you need additional help, please talk with one of the counselors at New Life Treatment Centers. The call is confidential and free.

1-800-NEW-LIFE
